The Davy Crockett Almanac and Book of Lists

WILLIAM R. CHEMERKA

EAKIN PRESS 🎭 Austin, Texas

Published in the United States of America
By Eakin Press
A Division of Sunbelt Media, Inc.
P.O. Drawer 90159 ⌨ Austin, Texas 78709-0159
email: eakinpub@sig.net
⌨ website: www.eakinpress.com ⌨

1   2   3   4   5   6   7   8   9

1-57168-319-4

Library of Congress Cataloging-in-Publication Data

Chemerka, William R.
    The Davy Crockett almanac and book of lists / by William R. Chemerka.
        p.   cm.
    Includes bibliographical references and index.
    ISBN 1-57168-319-4
    1. Crockett, Davy, 1786-1836 Miscellanea.   2. Crockett, Davy, 1786-1836--Influence.
3. Pioneers—Tennessee Biography.   4. Tennessee Biography.   5. Legislators--United
States Biography.   I. Title.
F436.C95C47   1999
976.8'04'092--dc21
    [B]   99-35289
                                                                                 CIP

This book is dedicated to
Fess Parker,
who is still the "King of the Wild Frontier."

FROM THE AUTHOR

The Davy Crockett Almanac & Book of Lists features three main sections: 1) an "Introduction" which traces the life and legend of Davy Crockett, 2) an "A" to "Z" section which contains historical and popular culture entries ranging from "*A Narrative of the Life of David Crockett of the State of Tennessee*" to "David Zucker," the motion picture director-producer who has featured a number of Crockett touches in his movies, and 3) the "Lists" section.

Many of the "A" to "Z" section's entries are cross-referenced, especially those relating to authors and their respective book titles. Secondary accounts of Crockett's life which appear in books about the Alamo, however, are not included in this work, despite some exceptions. For the most part, the thousands of periodical articles written about Crockett are not included in this work as separate entries in the "A" to "Z" section.

A number of entries and images in this book first appeared in *The Alamo Journal,* the official publication of The Alamo Society. A complete set of *The Alamo Journal* is held at the Daughters of the Republic Library at the Alamo in San Antonio, Texas. Anyone interested in a subscription to *The Alamo Journal* can contact this author in care of the publisher.

The author welcomes comments, corrections, clarifications and, above all, additions to *The Davy Crockett Almanac & Book of Lists.* Please contact the author c/o Eakin Press, P. O. Drawer 90159, Austin, Texas 78709-0159.

WILLIAM R. CHEMERKA

CONTENTS

Preface   vii
Acknowledgments   ix
Introduction: The Crockett of History   1
                The Crockett of Popular Culture   33
David Crockett Chronology   43
Crockett Family Tree   53
Crockett from "A" to "Z"   57
Crockett Numbers   143
Crockett Lists: 149
   Top Ten Crockett Books   150
   Top Dozen Davy Crockett Books for Kids   152
   Top Ten Questions/Comments Asked About
      David Crockett at the Alamo   155
   Top Ten Questions/Most Frequently Asked
      at the Crockett Tavern Museum   157
   Best Crockett Almanac Titles   159
   Crockett's Congressional Peers From Tennessee   160
   Davy Crockett's First Railroad Journey   161
   Author Comments About David Crockett   163
   Davy Crockett in the Movies   165
   Fess Parker's Top Ten Most Memorable Scenes
      From *Davy Crockett, King of the Wild Frontier*   168
   David Zucker's Crockett Touches in His Films   170
   Frank Thompson's "Davy Awards"   172
   Top Ten Crockett Food & Drink Items   176
   The Davy Crockett Drive-In   178
   Davy Crockett—An Idyl of the Backwoods   179
   Davy Crockett; Or; be Sure You're Right, Then Go Ahead   180

Davy Crockett Comic Books   181
Howard Bender's Top Ten Favorite
    Davy Crockett Comic Books   183
Howard Bender's Five Rarest
    Davy Crockett Comic Books   186
Murray Weissmann's Top Ten Disney
    Davy Crockett Collectibles   186
Paul DeVito's Top Ten Non-Disney
    Davy Crockett Collectibles   189
Davy Crockett and "The Simpsons"   191
Davy Crockett's Titles in "The Ballad of
    Davy Crockett"   192
Davy Crockett Shows up in the Strangest Places   193
"Crockett by Firelight"   195
David Crockett's Possessions at the Alamo   197
Past Presidents of the Direct Descendants of
    David Crockett   199
Crockett in the School Books   199
Descriptions of David Crockett   201
Other Published Deaths of Davy Crockett   202
Conclusion   210
Select Bibliography   211

PREFACE

Davy Crockett was but one man, although one author suggests that there were as many as six Crocketts! There is, of course, the Crockett of historical record who was born in Tennessee in 1786, fought in the Creek Indian War, served three terms in the United States House of Representatives, and fought and died at the Alamo in 1836. Most accounts refer to him as David Crockett. And there is the Crockett of legend, a larger-than-life figure who has been celebrated in book, song, poem, art, and film. In these accounts, he is usually referred to as Davy Crockett.

Who then was Davy Crockett?

In fact, the real Davy Crockett has been hard to define. Was he the "half-horse/half-alligator" Indian fighter who killed 105 bears in one hunting season and waded across the Mississippi River on a pair of wooden stilts? Or was he an inarticulate representative of poor canebrake squatters who, like him, saw the Western horizon as a place of economic opportunity?

Perhaps Crockett was a little of both.

Was he a self-promoting politician who knew the value of a good joke, or was he a genuine democrat who fought for those citizens who lacked a voice in government?

Perhaps Crockett exploited laughter's dividends to further the cause of the disadvantaged.

Was he the quintessential common man of the Jacksonian Era, or was he a calculating politician who served Nicholas Biddle and the Second National Bank of the United States?

Perhaps Crockett was atypically uncommon.

In any event, this book allows readers to explore the life and legend of Davy Crockett. For a more thorough understanding of the famous frontier hero, it is suggested that readers investigate some of the identified biographies that are highlighted in *The Davy Crockett Almanac & Book of Lists*.

WILLIAM R. CHEMERKA
August 1999

ACKNOWLEDGEMENTS

As I stated in the acknowledgements of *The Alamo Almanac & Book of Lists,* any book that calls itself a compilation, an anthology, a collection, or a "book of lists," must recognize and acknowledge all of those titles, whether they are books, films, songs, or other artistic creations, which were used as useful resources. As such, this volume is organized in such a way as to identify those individuals who added to the larger-than-life story of Davy Crockett. This book identifies many of them; however, the reader should seek out their original works for a more comprehensive appreciation of the legendary frontiersman.

In researching, collecting, and organizing appropriate information for this book, a number of individuals who were helpful immediately come to mind. Once again, the staff of the Daughters of the Republic of Texas (DRT) Library at the Alamo in San Antonio was particularly helpful in providing me with assistance during my visits over the last few years. Research assistant Sally Koch, Librarian Nancy Skokan, Library Assistant III Linda Edwards, Librarian Jeanette Phinney, Assistant Library Director Martha Utterback, and Library Director Elaine Davis were all generous with their time. Dorothy Reed Black of the DRT gathered the wonderful questions that so many of the Alamo's visitors posed to her during her tenure at the information center inside the Shrine of Texas Liberty. And curator Dr. Bruce Winders was kind enough to provide me with inventory inquiries during my most recent sojourn to the Alamo.

John Anderson, Preservations Officer, Archives & Information Services Division of the Texas State Library and Archives Commission in Austin, Texas, was most helpful in allowing me to secure several important images of David Crockett for this book.

The Direct Descendants of David Crockett (DDDC) played a very important role in helping me secure essential genealogical information that formed the foundation of the Crockett family tree. In particular, Francis John and Joy Bland, both past presidents of the growing organization, deserve special mention for their assistance.

I am indebted to Tennesseans Tim McCurry, Jim Claborn and Joe Swann, who shared their unique understanding of Crockett's early years with me while I attended the DDDC Family Reunion in Johnson City, Tennessee. I also thank Jim Claborn for the fine powder horn that he made for me. Joe Swan was kind enough to let me examine Crockett's first rifle, which he owns. To be sure, it was quite a thrill to hold one of Crockett's rifles. McCurry was thoughtful to serve as my personal tour guide at the Crockett Tavern. He also provided an interesting list of questions that have been frequently asked at the historic site.

Of course, members of the Alamo Society have been particularly helpful. Dr. Murray Weissmann not only contributed a unique roster to the "Lists" section but allowed me to examine his awesome collection of Crockett memorabilia. Since we "only live 40 miles apart," Dr. Weissmann was readily available to answer my many inquiries.

Paul DeVito also contributed a one-of-a-kind entry to the "Lists" section. His immense collection of Crockett memorabilia served as a unique resource to this volume. DeVito responded to numerous inquiries about the Crockett marketing phenomenon of the 1950s.

Frank Thompson, an accomplished film historian, contributed the "Davy Awards" section, a wonderful fact 'n' fun-filled addition about the celluloid adventures of Davy Crockett.

Film director-producer David Zucker's affection for Crockett is so genuine that he frequently embellishes his films with images and items relating to the famous frontiersman. He was kind enough to update those "Crockett Touches" in this volume.

And thanks to Ray Herbeck, Jr., the Associate Producer of *Alamo . . . The Price of Freedom,* who gave me the line "Crockett,

North Wall! Crockett!" in the 1988 IMAX motion picture. His decision allowed me to probably be the first actor in the history of the Screen Actors Guild whose first on-screen word was "Crockett."

Dr. Floyd Collins of Quincy University created a splendid original poem for this book. He also contributed information for the "A" to "Z" section.

A number of Alamo Society members contributed illustrations to this book. These artists include Howard Bender, Michael Boldt, John Bourdage, Rod Timanus, and the highly-regarded military artist Gary Zaboly. Some of these artists created original works for this book; others created Crockett images which had been previously published in *The Alamo Journal*, the official publication of The Alamo Society.

Other Alamo Society members who made contributions include Bill Groneman, Jim Simmons, John Berky, Roger Ross, Phil Riordan, Glenn Nolan, Jeff Bearden, Dr. Todd Harburn, and "Texas" Bob Reinhardt. My apologies to any other Alamo Society member whom I have overlooked.

Documentary director/producer Gary Foreman was kind enough to supply me with a number of Crockett almanac images which were quite useful. Gary gave me my first professional opportunity to portray Davy Crockett at the Witte Museum in San Antonio, Texas, in 1986.

And thanks to artist David Wright who patiently listened to my many Crockett stories during breaks in location shooting while on the set of Gary Foreman's "Frontier" History Channel series film site.

Thanks also to Abby Berenbak and the 1998-1999 United States History I Honors class at Madison High School in Madison, New Jersey, for their efforts. Technical assistance was kindly provided by Mark H. Nestor, Coordinator of Technology and Special Projects, Madison Public Schools.

My gratitude to the staff at Eakin Press for once again encouraging me to write this book. A special thank you to editor Robert F. Malina whose questions and concerns helped improve my original manuscript.

As always, thanks to my wife, Deborah, for so many things.

Finally, thanks to Fess Parker, who took time out on a Labor

Day not too long ago to recall his favorite memories from *Davy Crockett, King of the Wild Frontier.* I first met Fess Parker in San Antonio, Texas, in 1986. He allowed me to conduct a two-part interview with him for *The Alamo Journal* and he was kind enough to conduct a question-and-answer column called "Talkin' With Fess," that graced the pages of *The Alamo Journal* for a number of years that followed. I thoroughly enjoyed talking with him by phone before each issue went to press. I met him again at David Zucker's 1991 "Crockett Rifle Frolic" in California where we had a wonderful conversation about a wide range of topics, including, of course, Davy Crockett. Fess Parker was most gracious in accepting my invitation to be the guest of honor at the 1994 Alamo Society Symposium in San Antonio where he spoke and sat for hours signing autographs and posing for photographs. He made every Alamo Society member feel most welcome. We again met later that year in New York City, where he was hosting a wine tasting with some of his excellent Fess Parker Wines.

Fess Parker actually provided the initial spark which culminated in this book, although the entire process took several decades. His characterization of Crockett in "Davy Crockett at the Alamo," which was first broadcast on February 23, 1955, inspired me. I became a student of history because of that television production, and later graduated college as a history major. I have taught American History for twenty-eight years and have always managed to include lessons on David Crockett.

Again, thanks to those individuals who made *The Davy Crockett Alamanc & Book of Lists* a reality.

"Go ahead."

INTRODUCTION

THE CROCKETT OF HISTORY

This then is the heritage of pioneer experience—a passionate belief that a democracy was possible which should leave the individual a part to play in free society and not make him a cog in a machine operated from above; which trusted in the common man, in his tolerance, his ability to adjust differences with good humor, and to work out an American type from the contributions of all nations—a type for which he would fight against those who challenged it in arms, and for which in time of war he would make sacrifices, even the temporary sacrifice of individual freedom and his life lest that freedom be lost forever.

Frederick Jackson Turner

I leave this rule for others when I am dead. Be always sure you are right—then go ahead.

David Crockett

David Crockett was one of the most interesting individuals in American history. Born amidst the pervasive rural poverty that characterized the Appalachian frontier in the late eighteenth century, Crockett matured in the backwoods as a hunter, itinerant laborer, and Indian fighter. He served terms in the Tennessee state legislature and the United States House of Representatives, wrote an autobiography and became a celebrity of

1

"David Crockett" painting by William Henry Huddle, 1889.
— Courtesy of Texas State Library & Archives Commission

sorts in his own lifetime. His death as a member of the Alamo garrison in 1836 only strengthened the image of the "Go-Ahead" man.

Crockett was born on August 17, 1786, to John and Rebecca Crockett in eastern Tennessee where the Limestone Creek flows into the Nolichucky River. Young David was the fifth of nine Crockett children. "My father and mother had six sons and three daughters," stated Crockett in his 1834 autobiography, *A Narrative of the Life of David Crockett of the State of Tennessee.*

> **By the Creeks, my grandfather and grandmother Crockett were both murdered, in their homes, and on the very spot of ground where Rogersville, in Hawkins County, now stands.**

In his early years, the frontier itself was more of a menace to young David and his family than the Indians. In his autobiography, Crockett recalled an incident where he and his four older brothers and a friend nearly tumbled over a waterfall in a canoe before being rescued by a neighbor. And after the Crocketts moved to Cove Creek, Tennessee, in 1794, a flood destroyed the mill that John Crockett and partner Thomas Galbreath had built.

> **Away went their mill, shot, lock, and barrel. I remember the water rose so high, that it got into the house we lived in, and my father moved us out of it, to keep us from being drowned.**

Two years later, the Crocketts pulled up stakes again.

> **My father again removed, and this time settled in Jefferson County, now in the state of Tennessee; where he opened a tavern on the road from Abbingdon to Knoxville.**

The tavern catered primarily to teamsters. However, the number of wagoners who passed by the tavern were not numerous enough to generate adequate income for the struggling family. As a result, the Crocketts found themselves once again in poor financial straits.

> *I began to make up my acquaintance with hard times, and a plenty of them.*

David, now twelve years old, was hired out to drover Jacob Siler. But the pre-teen was no child; as a matter fact, he was a strong and agile boy, tempered by the physical challenges of the frontier. After completing a 400-mile journey to Virginia, the cattleman offered young David some money to remain with him, but the homesick Crockett was reluctant to stay with the man he called the "old Dutchman."

> *But home, poor as it was, again rushed on my memory, and it seemed ten times as dear to me as it ever had before. The reason was, that my parents were there; and there my anxious little heart panted to be.*

Young Crockett weathered a driving snowstorm and joined up with several teamsters who were heading back to Tennessee. Within a year of his return home, Crockett was enrolled in Benjamin Kitchen's "little country school." Frontier education was rudimentary at best. Inadequately trained teachers and one-room school houses filled with students of different ages and abilities did not positively contribute to the learning process. Nevertheless, Crockett attempted to master the basics of fundamental reading and writing. However, a fight with a fellow student caused the thirteen-year-old to circumvent school for several days because he feared a whipping from Kitchen. When the school master wrote Crockett's father about his son's extended absence, the elder Crockett threatened to whip David "an eternal sight worse than the master." David avoided his father's wrath by running away from home. He sojourned from the fall of 1799 to the spring of 1802 throughout Virginia and Maryland working as a hired hand, primarily with various teamsters.

Eventually, Crockett returned home yet again.

*I had been gone so long, and had grown so
much, that the family did not at first know me.*

Although the teenage Crockett had changed, his family's
fortunes had not. Debt was still the cornerstone of the Crockett
family. Among John Crockett's outstanding debts were sums of
$36 owed to Abraham Wilson and $40 owed to John Kennedy.
David worked as a six-month laborer for both Wilson and
Kennedy to pay off his father's debts.

*I concluded it was my duty as a child to help
him along, and ease his lot as much as I could.*

Following his initial work service, Crockett returned to Kennedy for another labor-intensive ordeal.

*I had worked a year without getting any
money at all, and my clothes were nearly
all worn out, and what few I had left were
mighty indifferent.*

While working for Kennedy in 1803, he fell in love with his
employer's niece. However, the "young woman from North Carolina" told Crockett that she was engaged to one of Kennedy's
sons. David seemingly suffered from his first broken heart.

*This news was worse to me than war, pestilence,
or famine; but still I knowed I could not help
myself.*

In his autobiography, Crockett acknowledged that "all of
my misfortunes growed out of my want of learning." Determined, he dedicated himself to mastering the fundamentals of
literacy. He enrolled at a school operated by a neighboring
Quaker.

*I proposed to him that I would go to school four
days in the week, and work for him the other two,
to pay my board and schooling. He agreed I might*

> *come on those terms; and so I went, learning and working back and forwards, until I had been with him nigh on six months. In this time I learned to read a little in my primer, to write my own name, and to cypher some in the three first rules in figures.*

During his stay at the school, Crockett fell in love with Margaret Elder, and the couple became engaged. To be sure, frontier engagements lacked the formality of those in the eastern seaboard cities. Backwoods "understandings" between sweethearts were rather informal agreements, usually lacking an engagement ring or formal acknowledgements by the respective families. Nevertheless, a Crockett-Elder union seemed certain, at least in the eyes of the young frontiersman. However, the engagement was terminated when she decided to marry someone else.

> *My heart was bruised, and my spirits were broken down; so I bid her farewell, and turned my lonesome and miserable steps back again homeward, concluding that I was only born for hardships, misery and disappointment.*

Crockett was seemingly so heartbroken that he viewed his future in the most pessimistic of romantic terms.

> *I now began to think, that in making me, it was entirely forgotten to make my mate; that I was born odd, and should always remain so, and that nobody would have me now.*

Crockett's lamentations, however, ended when Mary "Polly" Finley entered his life. The two met at a community frolic and they quickly took a liking to each other. However, the courtship was not a smooth one. Polly's mother did not endorse the developing relationship because she favored another young suitor.

> *Her mother was deeply enlisted for my rival,*
> *and I had to fight against her influence as*
> *well as his.*

After an absence of about two weeks David and Polly crossed paths by chance in the woods. During a wolf hunt, David got separated from the rest of the hunters in his party.

> *I went ahead, though, about six or seven*
> *miles, when I found night was coming on*
> *fast; but at this distressing time I saw a little*
> *woman streaking it along through the woods*
> *like all wrath, and so I cut on too, for I was*
> *determined I wouldn't lose sight of her that*
> *night any more. She had been out hunting*
> *her father's horses, and had missed her way.*

In his autobiography, Crockett recalled that "she looked sweeter than sugar." About a month after the encounter in the woods, David decided that he wanted Polly to be his wife. The young frontiersman, however, acknowledged that convincing Polly's parents, especially her mother, was going to be a difficult task. Crockett traveled to the Finley home to ask for Polly's hand in marriage.

> *When I got there, the old lady appeared to be*
> *mighty wrathy; and when I broached the sub-*
> *ject, she looked at me as savage as a meat*
> *axe. The old man appeared quite willing, and*
> *treated me very clever.*

Despite Mrs. Finley's reluctance to have David as a son-in-law, her husband persuaded her to condone the marriage. The couple were wed on August 16, 1806, one day before Crockett's twentieth birthday.

> *We worked on for some years, renting ground*
> *and paying high rent, until I found out it*
> *wasn't the thing it was cracked up to be; and*
> *that I couldn't make a fortune at it just at all.*

The Crockett's, now four in number with the birth of John Wesley in 1807, and William in 1809, moved again during the early autumn of 1811 to the head of the Mulberry Fork on the Elk River in Lincoln County, Tennessee. Crockett saw this particular juncture in his life as significant.

> *It was here that I began to distinguish myself as a hunter, and to lay the foundation for all my future greatness.*

The flintlock rifle was the primary firearm of the frontier. A qualified marksmen who could successfully secure game would be able to provide a subsistence existence for himself and his family. Of course, the muzzleloading rifle also offered an element of protection that was crucial to the backwoods family. Crockett recalled a number of hunting treks in his 1834 autobiography, many taking place during his childhood and teenage years.

After about a year, the Crockett's moved yet once more, settling on the Bean Creek in Franklin County, some ten miles south of Winchester, Tennessee. On November 25, 1812, Margaret Finley Crockett was born. But the peaceful isolation of their frontier home was soon broken by international events.

For several years the British had harassed American shipping as the young nation traded with France, which was at war with Great Britain. "British ships have continually violated the American flag on the great highway of nations, and have seized and carried off persons sailing under its protection," stated President James Madison on June 1, 1812, in a message to Congress.

The Indian problem on the frontier increased the tensions between the United States and Great Britain. A year earlier, the Shawnee chief, Tecumseh, initiated a confederation of tribes which battled an army led by Gen. William Henry Harrison, the governor of the Indiana Territory. "In this warfare, both women and children are killed and the Indians use brutal fighting methods," added Madison in his congressional message. "It is difficult to account for the activity among tribes in constant communication with British traders and garrisons without connecting their hostility with that influence." On June 18, 1812, The United States declared war against Great Britain.

Tennessee was essentially removed from military operations during the first year of fighting. In late 1812 and early 1813, most of the fighting took place along the United States-Canadian border, particularly around the eastern Great Lakes. Battle sites like Fort Dearborn, Michilimackinac, Ogdensburg, Queenston Heights, and Raisin River must have sounded foreign to those backwoods families who learned of the widening hostilities in the north. However, the war came south when the Creek Indians attacked Fort Mimms in what is now Alabama on August 30, 1813. The assault followed a massacre of Creeks weeks earlier at Burnt Corn Creek.

> *For when I heard of the mischief which was done at the fort, I instantly felt like going, and I had none of the dread of dying that I expected to feel.*

Crockett volunteered for a ninety-day term of service as a private on September 24, 1813, in Captain Francis Jones' Company of Tennessee Volunteer Mounted Riflemen.

> *The time arrived; I took a parting farewell of my wife and little boys, mounted my horse, and set sail, to join my company.*

Crockett extended the family tradition of military service that began with his father, a veteran of the Battle of King's Mountain in South Carolina on October 7, 1780. The battle was a significant victory for the American backwoodsmen over Major Patrick Ferguson's loyalist force during the Revolutionary War. But by 1812, many of the heroes of the Revolution had died: George Washington, Daniel Morgan, Alexander Hamilton, Benjamin Franklin, Patrick Henry, and John Hancock, to name a few. The war with Great Britain in 1812 provided a new generation of Americans with an opportunity to strike a blow against King George III.

> *At last we mustered about thirteen hundred strong, all mounted volunteers, and all determined to fight, judging from myself, for I felt wolfish all over.*

Crockett joined an expedition into Creek territory under Major John H. Gibson during the early autumn of 1813.

> *He came to my captain, and asked for two of his best woodsmen, and such as were best with a rifle. The captain pointed me out to him, and said he would be security that I would go as far as the major would himself, or any other man.*

The other recommended woodsman was George Russell. The pair, along with three other men, took part in a scouting trek into the Alabama Territory searching for Creek war parties. Gibson and six other volunteers undertook a similar foray into the wilderness. Crockett's squad discovered the whereabouts of the Creeks and quickly reported to Col. John Coffee's head-quarters stationed near modern-day Huntsville. Crockett arrived a day before Gibson and presented his scouting report to Coffee. However, Crockett was upset that Coffee needed confirmation of his findings.

> *When I made my report, it wasn't believed, because I was no officer; I was no great man, but just a poor soldier. But when the same thing was reported by Major Gibson!! why, then, it was all true as preaching, and the colonel believed it every word.*

This incident increased Crockett's animosity towards the officer corps of the United States Army, a posture which he maintained throughout his life. To be sure, his feelings were not particularly different from his backwoods peers. From the perspective of the trans-Appalachian farmer, the free-spirited frontier individual was the antithesis of the uniformed officer in the standing army. Crockett acknowledged that these differences had to be set aside because a war was raging on the frontier.

Colonel Coffee immediately informed his superior, Gen. Andrew Jackson, who was camped some forty miles away, about the status of his military operations to date. Following a forced march, Jackson, who was known as "Old Hickory" for his toughness, arrived at Coffee's new camp along the Tennessee River on October 10, 1813.

Within a month of Jackson's arrival, Crockett was engaged in several military operations against the Creeks. The first drive resulted in the destruction of a recently-abandoned Indian town on the Black Warrior River, near modern day Tuscaloosa, Alabama. In the days that followed, Crockett was given permission to hunt since the existing provisions that Coffee and Jackson possessed had been exhausted. Thanks to Crockett's efforts, the soldiers' half-rations were supplemented by deer and hog meat.

By early November, Jackson was preparing a major offensive against the Creeks at Tallusahatchee. On November 3, 1813, Jackson divided his force into two divisions and commenced an attack against the Creek camp. The fighting was horrific. Hand-to-hand combat and volley firings in the open were compounded by ferocious fighting in some of the houses.

> *We now shot them like dogs; and the set the house on fire, and burned it up with the forty-six warriors in it. I recollect seeing a boy who was shot down near the house. His arm and thigh was broken, and that he was so near the burning house that the grease was stewing out of him.*

The Creeks were thoroughly defeated. One hundred and eighty-six warriors were killed and dozens more were taken prisoner. However, another sizable Creek force was situated some thirty miles to the south, outside Fort Talladega. Crockett and his fellow volunteers were soon marching south under Jackson.

> *When we arrived near the place, we met eleven hundred painted warriors, the very choice of the Creek nation. They had encamped near the fort, and had informed the friendly Indians who were in it, that if they didn't come out, and fight with them against the whites, they would take their fort and all their ammunition and provision.*

A furious fight took place resulting in the deaths of approximately 300 warriors. Seventeen men in Jackson's command were killed. Yet, the victory wasn't a complete success since many of the Creeks managed to escape.

> *They fought with guns, and also with their bows and arrows, but at length they made their escape through a part of our line, which was made up of drafted militia, which broke ranks, and they passed.*

About a month after the Battle at Fort Talladega, Crockett's enlistment expired. On Christmas eve 1813, after volunteering his services for three months and six days, Crockett left for home. His pay, which included extra money for his horse, totaled $65.65, although he was actually paid $65.59 for some reason or another.

While Crockett remained home with Polly and his sons, John Wesley and William, the brutal frontier struggle continued. On March 27, 1814, Jackson defeated the Creeks at the Battle of Horseshoe Bend in the Alabama Territory. Though some Creeks remained on the warpath, the southeastern-based tribe ceded nearly two-thirds of their lands in southern Georgia and the Mississippi Territory to the United States according to the August 9, 1814, Treaty of Fort Jackson.

But the larger conflict, the War of 1812, expanded when the British invaded the United States during the summer of 1814. In August, the British defeated American forces outside of Washington, DC, in the Battle of Blandensburg. By August 24, British forces entered the nation's capital and set fire to many of the large government buildings, including the Capitol and the president's mansion. A month later, however, American forces stopped a combined British land and sea assault against Baltimore. The successful defense of Fort McHenry in Baltimore is notable, of course, since it inspired Francis Scott Key to write the *Star Spangled Banner.*

Crockett reenlisted on September 28, 1814. He traveled from home and joined a large American force under Jackson at Pensacola on November 8, 1814, a day before a fleet of British ships departed from the harbor. The British had been supplying the Creeks with weapons and gunpowder. Shortly thereafter, Jackson was ordered to New Orleans where the British planned their final offensive of the war. Crockett, in Major Uriah Blue's regiment, marched to Fort Montgomery, near the site of the former Fort Mimms.

> *We had about one thousand men, and as part of that number, one hundred and eighty-six Chickasaw and Choctaw Indians with us.*

Several expeditions of Indian allies and frontier scouts took place over the following weeks of the early winter. However, the war with the British soon ended. The Treaty of Ghent on December 24, 1814, officially terminated the fighting, and the Battle of New Orleans on January 8,1815, ended it once and for all. Still, the so-called Indian threat on the frontier remained, but Crockett spent nearly all of his service time scouting and hunting.

> *As the army marched, I hunted every day, and would kill every hawk, bird, and squirrel that I could find.*

Although a number of Creek war parties remained in Spanish Florida and the Alabama Territory, large scale fighting ceased. Crockett ended his second military tour of service on March 27, 1815, as a fourth sergeant.

> *This closed my career as a warrior, and I am glad of it, for I like life now a heap better than I did then; and am glad all over that I lived to see these times, which I should not have done if I had kept fooling along in war, and got used up at it.*

The year 1815 finally brought an end to the hostilities in the region, but the Crockett family did not fully enjoy benefits of peace. Sometime that summer, Polly died.

> *But in this time, I met with the hardest trial which*

ever falls to the lot of man. Death, that cruel lev-eller of all distinctions, — to whom the prayers and tears of husbands, and of even helpless infan-cy, are addressed in vain, — entered my humble cottage, and tore from my children an affectionate good mother, and from me a tender and loving wife.

Crockett invited his younger brother's family to live with him for a while in order to help raise the three children, John Wesley, William, and Margaret. Crockett, however, realized that he "must have another wife."

Crockett, who had been elected a lieutenant in 32nd Regiment of the Tennessee militia on May 21, 1815, soon began courting Elizabeth Patton, twenty-seven, a widow whose husband had died in the Creek Indian War.

She had two small children, a son and a daugh-ter, and both quite small, like my own. I began to think, that as we were both in the same situ-ation, it might be that we could do something for each other; and I began to hint a little around the matter, as we were once and a while together.

Early in 1816 (or possibly in late 1815), Elizabeth Patton married David Crockett. By the late summer of 1816, the Crockett family grew again. Robert Patton Crockett was born on September 16. Rebecca Elvira Crockett was born on December 15, 1818, and Matilda Crockett was born on August 2, 1821.

Restless, adventurous, and seemingly always looking for a parcel of better land for himself and his family, Crockett went on a number of excursions into the forest primeval. The results weren't always satisfactory. On one sojourn with some neighbors into the Alabama Territory he collapsed from what was probably malaria. Taken to the nearby home of Jesse Jones, he remained in a particularly poor state of health for two weeks. His absence from his family was lengthy enough that Elizabeth feared for the worse. To be sure, Crockett recovered.

When I got back home, it was to the utter
astonishment of my wife; for she supposed I
was dead. My neighbours who had started
with me had returned and took my horse
home, which they had found with theirs; and
they reported that they had seen men who had
helped bury me; and who saw me draw my
last breath. I know'd this was a whapper of a
lie, as soon as I heard it.

The next year the Crocketts moved some eighty miles away "to a place called Shoal Creek," just northeast of modern Lawrenceburg. The location quickly became a popular area for other frontier families; as a matter of fact, the area developed so quickly that the county of Lawrence was created in October of 1817. A month later on November 25, the Tennessee state legislature authorized the creation of twelve justices of the peace for the area. Crockett was appointed to one of the positions.

When a man owed a debt, and wouldn't pay
it, I and my constable ordered our warrant,
and then he would take the man, and bring
him before me for trial. I would give judg-
ment against him, and then an order of an
execution would easily scare the debt out of
the man.

Tennessee required written documentation of all court proceedings handled by the justices. Crockett, though, was essentially illiterate. But he was determined to correct his writing deficiencies with "care and attention."

Crockett was seemingly even more determined to represent a growing constituency of backwoods folks who were rapidly populating the lands west of the Appalachians. His satisfactory performance as a soldier in the Creek Indian War and his service as a justice of the peace helped elevate his military rank from that of a volunteer private to the elected colonel of the county militia. In fact, within fours years of the Treaty of Ghent, which formally ended the War of 1812, Crockett had risen to the office of Town Commissioner in Lawrenceburg. In addition, he was appointed to several judicial bodies which, for example, reported on internal transportation improvements.

Crockett set his political sights on higher office. He resigned his local position of justice of the peace on November 1, 1819. On January 1, 1821, he resigned as town commissioner and sought a seat in the Tennessee legislature in the 1821 election.

Although Crockett fearlessly fought Indians and wild game, there was one thing that he was afraid of: public speaking.

> *The thought of having to make a speech made my knees feel mighty weak, and set my heart to fluttering almost as bad as my first love scrape with the Quaker's niece. But as luck would have it, these big candidates spoke nearly all day, and when they quit, the people were worn out with fatigue, which afforded me a good apology for not discussing the government.*

Crockett's campaign strategy during the summer of 1821 was simple: speak for a short time, "tell a laughable story, and quit." It was a plan that seemed somewhat inappropriate, even for frontier voters. Nevertheless, Crockett won. But his superficial elementary political posture was augmented by an assortment of more substantial qualities, including honesty, dedication, determination, and a willingness to represent his constituency in a trustworthy manner.

In his first term in the state legislature, which began on September 21, 1821, Crockett assumed a more serious posture than the one he maintained during his jocular campaign of months earlier. He was most concerned with lands rights, particularly those of poor West Tennesseans from the canebrake.

During the fall term of the Fourteenth Tennessee General Assembly, Crockett was active in protecting the rights of the poor squatters by voting for a number of bills that would protect them against additional taxes and state claims to their lands. Although Crockett represented Hickman and Lawrence Counties, he had a genuine concern for all the poor working landowners of his state. Ironically, Crockett's own personal wealth, limited as it was, was dealt a severe blow when several of his business enterprises were destroyed during his first weeks in the legislature.

*I had built an extensive grist mill, and pow-
der mill, all connected together, and also a
large distillery. They had cost me upwards
of three thousand dollars, more than I was
worth in the world. The first news that I
heard after I got to the Legislature, was,
that my mills were — not blown up sky high,
as you would guess, by my powder establish-
ment, — but swept away all to smash by a
large fresh, that came soon after I left home.*

Despite the damage caused by the flood, Crockett was determined to pay off all his outstanding business debts.

*And so, you see, I determined not to break full
handed, but thought it better to keep a good
conscience with an empty purse, than to get a
bad opinion of myself, with a full one.*

After he returned to the legislature, he decided to move yet
again. Joined by his eldest son, John Wesley, and a young friend,
Abram Henry, Crockett explored northwest Tennessee and
claimed a parcel of land by the Obion River that was rich with
game. With the additional assistance of some river boatmen,
Crockett cleared some land, built a log cabin, planted corn, and
erected a rail fence.

Crockett returned to the state legislature for a special session called by Gov. William Carroll on April 22, 1822. He became involved in a number of land bills during the legislature's
regular session which commenced on July 22, 1822.

*I attended it, and served out my time, and
then returned, and took my family and what
plunder I had, and moved to where I built my
cabin, and made my [crop].*

Crockett, however, found himself campaigning for another
term in the Tennessee state legislature when his name was
thrown into the political ring. Although he had initially declined

to run when the idea was presented to him, Crockett actively campaigned for a legislative seat in 1823 against several candidates, including Dr. William Butler. Butler, who married one of Andrew Jackson's niece's, was an able opponent. But Crockett exploited Butler's formal education and successful socioeconomic status by emphasizing his own backwoods situation. The strategy, of course, was designed to cater to those in the electorate who viewed Butler as a kind of eastern elitist, one incapable of identifying with Crockett's frontier constituency.

> *I would therefore have me a large buckskin hunting-shirt made, with a couple of pockets holding about a peck each; and that in one I would carry a great big twist of tobacco, and in the other my bottle of liquor; for I knowed when I met a man and offered him a dram, he would throw out his quid of tobacco to take one, and after he had taken his horn, I would out with my twist and would give him another chaw.*

When the votes were counted, Crockett won hands down. On September 15, 1823, Crockett traveled to Murfreesborough, where he represented the counties of Carroll, Henderson, Humphreys, Madison, and Perry in Tennessee's Fifteenth General Assembly.

Again, Crockett's early legislative concern was for those poor squatters who had little or no voice in the general assembly. However, he was unsuccessful securing legislation that would protect the struggling farmers against those wealthier landholders and speculators who associated themselves with Andrew Jackson.

Although still a general supporter of "Old Hickory," Crockett's political parting with Andrew Jackson developed in this first legislative session. He voted for Col. John Williams against Jackson in the general assembly's vote for U.S. senator, a position Jackson won but later withdrew from.

> *I thought the colonel had honestly discharged his duty, and even the mighty name of Jackson*

couldn't make me vote against him. But voting against the old chief was found a mighty up-hill business to all of them except myself. I never would, nor never did, acknowledge I had voted wrong; and I am more certain now that I was right than ever. I told the people it was the best vote I ever gave; that I had supported the public interest, and cleared my conscience in giving it, instead of gratifying the private ambition of a man.

Crockett also supported the Second Bank of the United States, the financial institution which Jackson later opposed as president. The bank, which was chartered in 1816 during James Madison's last full year in office, was viewed by Jackson and others as an unconstitutional "money power," which favored "the rich and powerful." Crockett's support of Col. John Williams and the bank became the foundation of his political feud with Jackson.

The second session of the Tennessee General Assembly opened on September 20, 1824. Crockett, now representing ten counties, was active in promoting a number of bills, from transportation improvements to the protection of squatters.

In 1824, Andrew Jackson ran for president against several candidates. "Old Hickory" won more electoral votes than any of his three opponents: John Q. Adams, Henry Clay, and William Crawford. However, Jackson's ninety-nine votes were not enough to win a majority in the electoral college. Subsequently, the House of Representatives decided the election, awarding John Quincy Adams the presidency in 1825.

Crockett also entered the national political arena in 1825, when he challenged Col. Adam Alexander for Tennessee's Western District seat in the United States House of Representatives. Alexander, the incumbent, was a formidable candidate with support from Jacksonians in the state. In his first congressional campaign, Crockett attempted to exploit Alexander's pro-tariff position, since frontier squatters would seemingly benefit little from tax revenue generated from imported goods. However, economic times were generally good in western Tennessee and the voters were pleased with Alexander's representative performance. Alexander defeated Crockett by a vote of 2,866 to 2,599. Crockett said in his 1834 autobiography that he attributed his defeat to Alexander's successful campaign.

> *For it was the year that cotton brought twenty-five dollars a hundred; and so Colonel Alexander would get up and tell the people, it was all the good effect of this tariff law; that it had raised the price of their cotton, and that it would raise the price of every thing else they made to sell.*

Following his defeat, Crockett attempted a commercial undertaking.

> *In the fall of 1825, I concluded I would build two large boats, and load them with pipe staves for market. So I went down to the lake, which was about twenty-five miles from where I lived, and hired some hands to assist me, and went to work; some at boat building, and others at getting staves. I worked on with my hands till the bears got fat, and then I turned out to hunting, to lay in a supply of meat.*

Crockett claimed to kill fifty-eight bears during the fall and winter of 1825-1826 and another forty-seven during the early spring of 1826, before heading down the Obion River with two boats of staves. His goal was to sail to the Mississippi River and travel all the way to New Orleans where he would sell his 30,000 staves. But his novice crew was unable to negotiate the Mississippi River. His boats crashed into some drift timber and began to sink. Although Crockett was below in one of the sinking boats, he managed to scramble to one of the small window-like openings and yell for help.

> *By a violent effort they jerked me through; but I was in a pretty pickle when I got*

> **through. I had been sitting without any cloth-
> ing over my shirt: this was torn off, and I was
> literally skin'd like a rabbit. I was, however,
> well pleased to get out in any way, even with-
> out shirt or hide.**

Crockett and his mates survived the crash but they were stranded on the drift timber until the next morning when they were rescued by a passing craft. Taken to Memphis, Crockett was clothed by Marcus B. Winchester, the city's postmaster. Winchester's humanitarianism towards Crockett was punctuated with suggestions that the former Tennessee legislator should consider running for Congress again.

By the summer of 1827, Crockett hit the campaign trail again. Running against him was Col. William Arnold and the incumbent, Col. Adam Alexander. Crockett's opponents, especially Alexander, had sizable campaign war chests. Crockett, who had been broke since the boat accident the previous year, was bankrolled with tidy sums from Winchester. Arnold and Alexander generally ignored Crockett's challenge; as a matter of fact, on a number of occasions both countered each other's claims on the campaign trail without even acknowledging Crockett's candidacy. However, Crockett emerged victorious winning with 5,868 votes to Alexander's 3,646 votes; Arnold tallied 2,417.

The Twentieth Congress convened on December 3, 1827. Among its newest members was the honorable David Crockett. True to his constituency, Crockett focused most of his energies on the Tennessee Vacant Land Bill, which was designed to allow Tennessee to sell vacant federal property within its borders. According to one of the bill's supporters, Tennessee's James Knox Polk, the land would benefit Tennessee best if it could be sold at a high price. Crockett initially supported Polk, but he questioned the impact of the bill on the poor squatters who would probably be forced off the land since they lacked the hard money to buy it. The bill was eventually tabled. The disagreement between Polk and Crockett over the land bill developed into something more serious than a topical debate: it created a split between Crockett and the Polk-led Tennessee Jacksonians.

Crockett won reelection in 1829 in grand style. He tallied

6,773 votes to Col. Adam Alexander's 3,641. Two additional candidates shared 168 other votes. In addition, Andrew Jackson had been inaugurated as president earlier in the year with his newly-named Democratic Party holding majorities in both houses of Congress. While Crockett still generally claimed to be a Jackson supporter, he carefully stated the limits of political loyalty.

> *I was willing to go with General Jackson in every thing that I believed was honest and right; but further than this, I wouldn't go for him, or any other man in the whole creation; that I would sooner be honestly and politically d__nd, than hypocritically immortalized.*

In the Twenty-first Congress, Crockett attempted to revive the tabled land bill but was unsuccessful. As a champion of the frontier poor, Crockett voted for internal transportation improvements, which he hoped would promote economic activity throughout western Tennessee. But Jackson vetoed a major piece of transportation legislation, the Maysville Road Bill. Although the bill was unique to Kentucky, Crockett saw the veto as a threat to future legislation which would benefit his own state. Crockett's unsuccessful effort to revive the bill only furthered the growing rift between him and Jackson.

Crockett also argued for the abolition of the United States Military Academy at West Point because he saw the institution favored the "sons of the rich and influential." His protests, of course, were unsuccessful. But by these political stands, Crockett established himself as a man of principle who was willing to challenge the leadership of his own party.

Crockett's greatest challenge to the Jacksonians concerned the Indian Resettlement Act, which was designed to move many of the Southeastern tribes west of the Mississippi River. The legislative practice of uprooting Native American tribes was not unique to the 1830s; in fact, the process had been going on for a considerable time in the early nineteenth century. Original treaties were altered in a number of ways, sometimes as the result of deception, at other times as a result of force. Nearly one hundred treaties were negotiated during Jackson's two terms alone. The Indian Resettlement Act was introduced on February 24, 1830.

> *I voted against this Indian bill, and my conscience yet tells me that I gave a good and honest vote, and one that I believe will not make me ashamed in the day of judgment.*

More than any other piece of legislation, Crockett's position on the Indian Resettlement Act reflected his principled character. To be sure, like all politicians he learned the art of compromise, but on major issues which he considered just, Crockett was uncharacteristically consistent. As a veteran of the Creek Indian War, one would assume that Crockett was not sympathetic to the indigenous people of the American Southeast. Furthermore, his grandparents had been killed by Indians during the Revolutionary War. But Crockett saw the forceable removal of the Indians as a moral wrong. Anti-Jackson forces in the northeast exploited Crockett's position by promoting a circular letter which described the frontiersman's charitable stance against his former adversaries. Surprisingly, however, no anti-Indian bill remarks by Crockett appear in the *Congressional Debates,* which traced the bill's fate until its passage on May 24, 1830. Nevertheless, the split between Crockett and Jackson seemed permanent.

Crockett's attempt to win a third term in the House of Representatives in 1831 was curbed by Jackson forces in Tennessee, particularly Madison County, where the influential *Jackson Gazette* was published. The campaign was a heated one; as a matter of fact, at one public debate his chief opponent, William Fitzgerald, drew a pistol on Crockett when the frontier politician approached him to challenge something he had said! Although Crockett received 7,948 ballots from the voters in the eighteen-county congressional district, Fitzgerald won 8,534 votes and the election. Crockett won a majority of the total vote from all counties except Madison, where Fitzgerald topped him 1,214 to 429.

In defeat, Crockett thanked the people who voted for him.

> *The people of the district, and of Madison county among the rest, seemed disposed to prove Mr.*

Fitzgerald and the Jackson Legislature, that they were not to be transferred like hogs, horses, and cattle in the market; and they determined that I shouldn't be broke down, though I had to carry Jackson, and the enemies of the bank, and the legislative works all at once.

Crockett returned to his home in Weakley County, Tennessee, following the adjournment of Congress on March 3, 1831. As usual, debts faced the former Congressman. On May 19, 1831, he was forced to sell some of his acreage and a slave to pay off a debt generated by a legal suit. Although not active in the national political arena, Crockett remained somewhat involved in local affairs. He served as a road commissioner, a juror and estate executor of his father-in-law's estate.

Andrew Jackson won reelection in the 1832 election, and managed to maintain a Democratic majority in the House of Representatives, but a loose coalition of National Republicans and other minor parties held a slight advantage in the Senate. Within two years most of the anti-Jackson forces would unite under the banner of the Whig Party. However, the Whigs lacked a leader with a national profile. To be sure, Crockett seemed to be such an appropriate individual, especially since he was Jackson's home-state nemesis. But Crockett needed the floor of Congress to launch a national challenge against Jackson. As such, Crockett sought victory in the congressional elections of 1833.

Crockett's race for the new Twelfth District seat against the incumbent William Fitzgerald was a difficult one. The pro-Jackson state legislature had gerrymandered the new district to include Madison County, which cost Crockett the election two years earlier. In addition to Fitzgerald's attacks, Jacksonian lawyer Adam Huntsman penned a number of newspaper tracts criticizing Crockett.

But a series of newspaper articles, in the form of fictional letters "written" by Maj. Jack Downing, assisted Crockett to an extent. The Downing letters were actually written by Seba Smith, a New England journalist who was eager to exploit the public's growing demand for frontier philosophy and cracker barrel wisdom. The fictional Downing wasn't a Tennessee backwoodsman but a product of the Maine countryside. To many in the northeast, Maine was somewhat more primitive than Crockett's home state. And it had joined the Union in 1820, some twenty-four years after Tennessee became the sixteenth state. Although the Downing character wasn't Crockett, there was enough similarity in the printed words to cause an innocuous confusion in the minds of some readers. In any event, people enjoyed the Crockett-like Downing letters, and Crockett benefited from the association.

Crockett, however, also had a literary boost thanks to Matthew St. Clair Clarke's 1833 book, *Life and Adventures of Colonel David Crockett of West Tennessee*. The book generously borrowed scripted lines from James Kirke Paulding's play *The Lion of the West*, which featured a larger-than-life fictional frontier persona named Nimrod Wildfire. Coincidentally, it was generally believed that Paulding based Wildfire on Crockett. In the book, Clarke attributed a brag-laden monologue to Crockett, which became associated with him forever: "I'm that same David Crockett, fresh from the backwoods, half-horse, half-alligator, a little touched with snapping turtle." Initially, Crockett criticized the volume as not being "genuine," but he later realized that the popular work had favorably spread his name. The book was regarded highly enough to spawn a second printing in 1833 under the title *Sketches and Eccentricities of Colonel David Crockett of West Tennessee*. It is not known, however, to what extent the volumes assisted Crockett in his campaign. Nevertheless, Crockett defeated Fitzgerald, 3,985 to 3,812.

By the time of his victory in 1833, Crockett had developed into a national figure more, to be sure, for his frontier exploits than for his political dealings. For example, in December, Crockett attended a Washington, DC, performance of *The Lion of the West*, which starred James Hackett in the Crockett-like title role. Like the publication of Matthew St. Clair Clarke's book, Crockett initially frowned upon the Hackett's characterization, but he soon warmed up to the production when he realized that it also promoted his national political posture. During the performance, Hackett, in full frontier costume, acknowledged Crockett, who stood up and reciprocated with a bow.

At this same time, Crockett was in the process of writing his autobiography with the help of Kentucky's Thomas Chilton, a friend since the frontiersman's first term in Congress. "I am engaged in writing a history of my life," Crockett wrote his son John on January 19, 1834. Less than a month later, Philadelphia publishers Carey and Hart issued commercial broadsides heralding the upcoming release from "this genuine Son of the West."

Crockett's autobiography, *A Narrative of the Life of David Crockett of the State of Tennessee,* was a well-received volume of the nation's most famous living frontier hero. Filled with lively backwood language, the book took liberties with some events in order to further the political possibilities of the three-term Congressman. Although his autobiography did not generate significant income for the debt-ridden Tennessean, it underscored a planned party-promoted tour for him of the northeast. In a letter dated April 9, 1834, to a friend, Hiram S. Favor, Crockett noted that he viewed the tour as an opportunity to see "merely for curiosity" a part of the nation that he was unfamiliar with.

The Whigs saw the tour as something more serious than "curiosity." As a matter of fact, some within the ranks of the Whig Party perceived Crockett as the logical choice to challenge Jackson or some other Democrat in the 1836 presidential election. Furthermore, a Mississippi convention formally asked Crockett to run for the nation's highest office. However, to others, Crockett lacked the sophistication to execute a successful presidential campaign since he had failed to have any legislation passed during his three terms in Congress.

In any event, Crockett began his speaking tour on April 25, 1834. He traveled from Washington, DC, to Baltimore, the birthplace of the Whig Party. He continued on to Philadelphia where the Young Whigs of the city informed him that they would be presenting him with a custom-made rifle later in the year. Crossing the Delaware River to Bordentown, Crockett boarded the Camden & Amboy Railroad for a journey across New Jersey to South Amboy where he sailed to Manhattan. He continued his political sojourn to Boston and Lowell, Massachusetts. The *Boston Transcript* noted that he addressed an audience with "a very happy speech of nearly half an hours duration—in which he expressed his gratitude for the unexpected honors which had been paid him." The article reported that Crockett went on to to criticize the Jackson "administration in terms of decided disapprobation."

Crockett concluded his tour by mid-May, but planned to return to Philadelphia on July 4, 1834, to receive his rifle. His return to the City of Brotherly Love on Independence Day marked the peak of his popularity. He was warmly greeted by enthusiastic crowds throughout the city; as a matter of fact, it was a kind of triumph only reserved for victorious military heroes or heads of state. After being presented the rifle by the Young Whigs, he later delivered a well-received speech at the Music Fund Hall. Noted Poulson's *American Daily Advertiser* three days after Crockett's speech: "The Hon. Member from Tennessee presented himself before his delighted auditors, and his usual unaffected and good humored manner, contributed to the gratification of the day."

But the northeast was not completely won over by the canebrake Congressman. For example, on July 1, 1834, New York's *Monroe Democrat* described him as "that grinning traitor of a Crockett." In addition, his attacks on the Jackson administration failed to generate the kind of band wagoning necessary to propel his candidacy beyond the limited Whig realm.

Debt continued to plague Crockett, but some wealthy Whigs, like Nicholas Biddle, president of the Second Bank of the United States, assumed some of his notes of indebtedness. The Whigs also promoted Crockett's national profile by generating such ghostwritten books as *Col. Crockett's Tour to the North and Down East* and the *Life of Martin Van Buren* in 1835, the year of the congressional elections. Furthermore, a song, "The Crockett Victory March," was published.

On the surface, it appeared that Crockett's reelection bid in 1835 was a sure thing since his popularity was seemingly at an all-time high. The various Crockett books, his tour of the northeast, and the first of a series of *Davy Crockett Almanacks* all contributed to the optimism which underscored his summer campaign. Even the widely-circulated *Nile's Weekly Register* admired him for his independence in the House of Representatives. "The vote is his own," proclaimed the publication. But the Jackson forces in Tennessee were determined to defeat Crockett. They realized that Crockett was vulnerable because his Whig support was not rock-solid; as a matter of fact, Crockett's attempt to revive his Tennessee Land Bill was viewed by some Whigs as parochial and not congruent to the national goals of the anti-Jacksonians. Nevertheless, Crockett went ahead.

Adam Huntsman, who had penned several unsuccessful anti-Crockett monographs during the 1833 congressional elections, opposed him in 1835. Crockett won 4,400 votes, but Huntsman won the election with 4,652 votes. On November 1, 1835, at the Union Hotel in Memphis, Crockett said to a small group of constituents: "Since you have chosen to elect a man with a timber toe to succeed me, you may all go to hell and I will go to Texas."

And so he did.

A revolution had broken out in Texas, which was then part of Mexico. In the 1820s, the Mexican government had encouraged Americans to settle in Texas with the promise of large tracts of inexpensive lands. Tens of thousands of Americans took advantage of the generous Mexican offer, but soon the Anglos outnumbered the native Mexican population. A Mexican decree in 1830 curbed further colonization from the United States, but the seeds of protest had already been planted by the likes of Stephen F. Austin and others. The Mexican government, under the dictatorship of Gen. Antonio Lopez de Santa Anna, suppressed all democratic protests by 1834. On October 2, 1835, the revolution began at Gonzales when armed Texians fired upon a Mexican cavalry unit that was attempting to confiscate an artillery piece. By the end of 1835, the Texas revolutionaries had forced all Mexican forces to retreat south of the Rio Grande River. Furthermore, a Texian General Council formed volunteer ranging companies and sought financial aid from U.S. citizens.

Crockett, forty-nine years old and wearing "that same veritable coon-skin cap and hunting shirt," departed Memphis with several associates for Texas. Crockett's original motive for heading to Texas was to "explore" the region. In a letter written in early January of 1836 to his oldest daughter, Margaret, and her husband, Crockett stated: "Texas is the garden spot of the world. The best land and the best prospects for health I ever saw, and I do believe it is a fortune to any man to come here."

In the letter, Crockett mentioned that he had "taken the oath of government and have enrolled my name as a volunteer." The oath originally stated that anyone who signed it would "bear true allegiance to the Provisional Government of Texas or any future government that may be hereafter declared." Crockett, however, fearful of any future government that might reject democratic principles, inserted the word "republican" after the word "future." Crockett saw a successful independent Texas as a way of reviving his political career. He noted to Margaret that: "I am in hopes of making a fortune yet for myself and family, bad as my prospect has been."

On January 12, 1836, Crockett was sworn into Capt. William B. Harrison's company in the Volunteer Auxiliary Corps of Texas at Nacogdoches. On January 23, he was in Washington-on-the-Brazos, getting provisioned. Shortly thereafter, Crockett and the volunteers journeyed to the southwest.

A few weeks later on February 5, Crockett arrived in San Antonio de Bexar, where William B. Travis and James Bowie commanded a companion force of regulars and volunteers. Despite Crockett's reputation, he offered to serve as a "high private."

Advance units of Santa Anna's army under General Ramirez y Sesma reached San Antonio on February 23. The Texians hastily retreated inside the Alamo, the mission-fortress situated several hundred yards outside of the town on the other side of the San Antonio River.

Immediately outnumbered, Travis sent out riders with pleas for help. His letter of February 24 is particularly memorable for its determination and spirit. "I shall never surrender or retreat," wrote Travis. "Victory or Death." In a letter dated February 25, Travis extolled Crockett as being "seen at all points, animating the men to do their duty."

During the siege, a small relief force arrived from Gonzales which increased the garrison's force to over 200 defenders. And a message dated March 1 from Maj. R. M. Williamson pledged a relief force numbering more than 600 men-at-arms. "For God's sake, hold out until we can assist you," stated Williamson.

But additional help did not come.

Unknown to Crockett and the Alamo defenders, delegates

to a General Convention at Washington-on-the-Brazos declared Texas an independent republic on March 2.

The birth date of the Republic of Texas was also unknown to Santa Anna. But such political details were irrelevant to the self-proclaimed "Napoleon of the West," who prepared a four-column infantry assault against the Alamo.

On the thirteenth day of the siege, Santa Anna's soldiers attacked the Alamo during a predawn attack on March 6, 1836. After an hour of desperate struggle, Crockett and the others lay dead. The exact location of where David Crockett made his last stand remains an unanswered question, although in all probability it was somewhere in or near the courtyard which fronted the entrance to the Alamo church. How Crockett died also remains an unanswered question.

Although all of the defenders were killed, one of the non-combatants, Mrs. Susannah Dickinson, stated that as she exited the Alamo church following the battle she "recognized Colonel Crockett lying dead and mutilated between the church and the two story barrack building, [his] peculiar cap by his side." According to Travis' slave, Joe, "Crockett and a few of his friends were found together with twenty-four of the enemy dead around them." On March 28, 1836, the *Louisiana Advertiser* declared that: "Col. Crockett is among the slain . . . [He] fell like a tiger."

On the other hand, a collection of pages attributed to José Enrique de la Peña, a Mexican officer who served under Santa Anna, suggests that Crockett was one of several defenders who were captured and executed after the battle: "Some seven men had survived the general carnage, and under the protection of General Castrillon, they were brought before Santa Anna. Among them . . . was the naturalist David Crockett, well known in North America for his unusual adventures. . . . Santa Anna answered Castrillon's intervention in Crockett's behalf with a gesture of indignation and, addressing himself to . . . the troops closest to him, ordered his execution. The commanders and officers were outraged at this action and did not support the order . . . ; but several officers who were around the president and who, perhaps, had not been present during the moment of danger . . . thrust themselves forward, . . . and with swords in hand, fell upon these unfortunate, defenseless men just as a tiger leaps upon his prey. Though tortured before they were killed, these unfortunates died without complaining and without humiliating themselves before their torturers."

Other accounts suggested that Crockett survived the siege and Battle of the Alamo. For example, on April 5, 1836, *The Monroe Democrat* erroneously printed on its front page that "We are happy to state, on the authority of a letter from Tennessee, that the report of the death of the eccentric Davy Crockett is not true."

David Crockett died on March 6, 1836. Along with the other Alamo defenders (save José Gregorio Esparza), his body was burned. The ashes of the defenders lay scattered; however, some of the ashes were saved and were ceremoniously interned under the direction of Col. Juan Seguin in San Antonio on February 25, 1837. Speaking in Spanish, Seguin paid homage to "our departed brethren, Travis, Bowie, Crockett."

The Legendary Davy Crockett, illustration by Howard Bender.

THE CROCKETT OF POPULAR CULTURE

"Born on a mountain top in Tennessee, Greenest state in the Land of the Free Raised in the woods so he knew every tree Kilt him a b'ar when he was only three, Davy Davy Crockett—King of the Wild Frontier"

"The Ballad of Davy Crockett"
© 1954 Wonderland Music Co., Inc.

Even before he died at the Alamo, David Crockett was a celebrated figure in the United States. His popularity was boosted by his autobiography in 1834, the first of the lively almanacs in 1835, the well-received stage play *The Lion of the West*, which debuted in 1831, and hundreds of newspaper accounts of his exploits. But after his death, Crockett became even a larger figure. In fact, Crockett has been continuously celebrated in song, book, play, poem, and film over the course of two centuries.

The Crockett of popular culture was firmly established by 1836, when Richard Penn Smith wrote another Crockett "autobiography," *Col. Crockett's Exploits and Adventures in Texas*. The book was supposedly a diary of sorts, in which Crockett penned his thoughts right up to the morning of March 6, 1836, when Santa Anna's soldiers stormed the Alamo. Hardly anyone knew that Crockett didn't write it, but it didn't matter. It sold well and was augmented by the growing popularity of the Crockett almanacs.

The Crockett almanacs, which were printed regularly until

1856, featured outrageous tales of the frontiersman taming wild animals, riding up Niagara Falls on an alligator, and battling comets! The 1837 *Almanack* described his death at the Alamo in near superhuman terms: "It was calculated that during the siege, he killed no less than 85 men, and wounded 120 besides, as he was one of the best shooters of the west, and he had four rifles, with two men to load constantly, and he fired as fast as they could load, nearly always hitting his man."

During the Civil War, Crockett's legend was overshadowed by the exploits of such individuals as Robert E. Lee, Ulysses S. Grant, Thomas "Stonewall" Jackson, and William T. Sherman, to name an obvious few. Nevertheless, Crockett remained in print thanks to the Beadle's Dime Biographical Library which published *Col. David Crockett, The Celebrated Hunter, Wit and Patriot* in 1861, and the *Life and Adventures of Colonel David Crockett* in 1864.

Following the War Between the States, Crockett appeared to yet another generation of Americans courtesy of new periodical articles and dramatic stage productions. An April 1867 Harper's *New Monthly Magazine* featured a six-page story titled "Davy Crockett's Electioneering Tour," and the play *Davy Crockett; or, Be Sure You're Right, Then Go Ahead,* debuted in 1872. The production ran until 1896, when its star, Frank Mayo, died. John S. C. Abbott wrote *David Crockett: His Life and Adventures* in 1874 for Dodd, Mead and Company's "American Pioneers and Patriots" series. Abbott said that "there is probably not an adult American, in all these widespread states, who has not heard of David Crockett." A year later, George Cary Eggleston penned *David Crockett.*

In 1883, Crockett was included in an article in the *Magazine of American History,* and a year later Edward S. Ellis wrote *The Life of Colonel David Crockett.* William F. Cody's *Story of the Wild West* in 1888 included Crockett along with other legendary frontier heroes.

According to historian Frederick Jackson Turner in his seminal 1893 Chicago address, the ever-changing frontier had created and maintained America's democratic and egalitarian character. He carefully described the first "moving mass" of settlers into the Piedmont region which included "the ancestors of John C. Calhoun, Abraham Lincoln, Jefferson Davis, Stonewall Jackson, James K. Polk, Sam Houston, and Davy Crockett . . ." But by the final decade of the nineteenth century, Turner's frontier had closed. Still, the public's interest in the frontier remained strong. To satisfy the public's demand, Buffalo Bill's Wild West shows and printed stories about George Custer, Annie Oakley, cowboy shoot-em-ups and the legend of Davy Crockett helped keep the spirit of the frontier alive.

By 1898, America was a world power. Its imperialistic victory in the Spanish American War spawned a new cadre of heroes, from Commodore George Dewey to Theodore Roosevelt. But the legend of Davy Crockett remained in the public arena as new books sprang from the presses.

1900-1919

In 1900, Frances M. Perry penned *The Story of David Crockett For Young Readers,* a title in the Baldwin's Biographical Booklet series. The new century witnessed the *The Life of David Crockett* in 1902, essentially a combined reprint of his autobiography and his ghostwritten Texas exploits. In 1905, Harriet G. Reiter wrote *David Crockett,* a thirty-one-page booklet in the Instructor Literature Series. Reiter's Crockett "stood alone like a lion at bay" in the final moments of her description of the famous frontiersman at the Alamo. In 1908, Edward Willett wrote *Davy Crockett's Boy Hunter,* a pulp reader in the popular Beadles Frontier Series, and Everett McNeil wrote In *Texas With Davy Crockett; A Story of the Texas War of Independence.* During the next year, a silent film titled *Davy Crockett—in Hearts United* premiered. Another silent film, simply called *Davy Crockett,* was released the next year.

1920s

In the 1920s several songs titled "Davy Crockett" were published, and Sunset Productions released the silent film *Davy Crockett at the Fall of the Alamo* in 1926, with Cullen Landis in the title role. The decade began with a feature story on Crockett in the February 1920 issue of *The Mentor: Pioneers of the Great West.* In 1921, Yale University Press published the multi-volume *The Chronicles of America Series.* Volume 24 of the series, *Texas and the Mexican War,* featured Homeric-like passages on the legendary backwoodsman: "David Crockett, who had come from his native Tennessee to throw in his lot with the Texans, sold his life amid the last massacre as grimly as a Norse Viking in an Icelandic saga." The Southern Pacific Railroad used Crockett's image to promote their passenger service. In 1928, the Boston-based John Hancock Insurance Company produced a sixteen-page booklet titled *David Crockett: Backwoodsman and Congressman.* The booklet stated: "We do not know how Davy Crockett died. Some think that he was among the last six survivors, that they surrendered and were taken before Santa Anna, who ordered that they be killed at once. But it is more probable that the brave woodsman died with his face to the foe, undaunted and resolute,—on his lips, the words—'Go Ahead.'" The decade ended with a Crockett cover story ("Davy Crockett, Hero and Congressman") in the May 1929 issue of *Frontier Times,* the publication that was "devoted to frontier history, border tragedy, and pioneer achievements."

1930s

In 1931, the New York-based Conqueror Records released vocalist Chubby Parker's "Davey Crockett." Lane Chandler played the famous frontiersman in Columbia Pictures' *Heroes of the Alamo* in 1937. Said film historian Frank Thompson of Chandler's performance: "Crockett is younger than he should be, but otherwise is a canny mixture of the historical and the legendary." In 1939, Robert Barratt portrayed Crockett in the Sam Houston bio-pic, *Man of Conquest,* which starred Richard Dix. Surprisingly, Barrat's Crockett is killed with a pistol in the film. Constance Rourke's 1934 book *Davy Crockett* was a unique volume, combining story telling with a interesting final chapter of the Crockett almanacs. Rourke was quite accurate when she stated: "About no single American figure have so many legends clustered." In 1938, Sterling Waters starred as Crockett in the narrated educational film *The Alamo: "Shrine of Texas Liberty."* A year later, Richard M. Dorson edited selections from the Crockett almanacs and published them as *Davy Crockett: American Comic Legend.*

1940s

The public's demand for Crockett material continued in the 1940s. For example, Frank Beals' *Davy Crockett* was published in 1941 as part of the Chicago-based Wheeler Publishing Company's "American Adventure Series." Also in 1941, Crockett appeared in the comic book *World Famous Heroes,* number one. To be sure, news of World War II dominated the readings of Americans between late 1941 and 1945, but that did not stop writers and publishers from delivering articles about David Crockett. In 1943, for instance, the April issue of *Encore* magazine featured an eleven-page article titled "Davy Crockett—The Siege of the Alamo." A year later, Irwin Shapiro wrote *Yankee Thunder: The Legendary Life of Davy Crockett,* and following the war in 1948, Crockett appeared at the Alamo in the comic book *Dead-Eye Western Comics,* number one. In 1949, Aileen W. Parks authored *Davy Crockett, Young Rifleman* and Crockett appeared in Commended Comics' *Tex Granger,* issue number twenty.

1950s

The most celebrated Crockett decade in the twentieth century was the 1950s, when Walt Disney produced a three-part series titled *Davy Crockett, King of the Wild Frontier* during the 1954-1955 television season. But early 1950s were filled with images and stories of Davy Crockett. In fact, the decade began with a Crockett film, *Davy Crockett—Indian Scout.* Although the Lew Landers-directed motion picture starred George Montgomery as a cousin of the famous Davy Crockett, it nevertheless maintained the popular culture tradition of the famous Alamo defender. The famous frontiersman was illustrated by artist Benton Clark on the cover of *Blue Book Magazine of Adventure in Fact and Fiction* in June 1951. The magazine included a story titled "Men of America—David Crockett." Furthermore, Avon Comics produced a single title called *Frontier Fighter Davy Crockett* in 1951. And the famous backwoodsman was featured in issue number six of *Indian Fighter,* also in 1951. Among the best books for young readers was Enid Lamonte Meadowcraft's *The Story of Davy Crockett,* published in 1952. Meadowcraft traced Crockett's life from his boyhood years to his death at the Alamo.

However, the Disney production dwarfs nearly every previous popular culture effort. The three chronologically-arranged, hour-long episodes became television's first mini-series. Starring Texas-born actor Fess Parker, the Disney series traced Crockett's adult life from the Creek Indian War in 1813, to his death at the Alamo in 1836. From the conclusion of the first episode, "Davy Crockett, Indian Fighter," on December 15, 1954, Disney realized that he had a huge hit on his hands, especially the episode's signature theme song, "The Ballad of Davy Crockett." The tune was covered by numerous artists, including Gabe Drake and the Woodsmen, Walter Schumann, Tex Ritter, Mitch Miller, Tennessee Ernie Ford, and Burl Ives, among others. One version on Cadence Records, sung by Bill Hayes, sold several million copies and topped the national record charts for five consecutive weeks. Even Fess Parker's version of the song sold a million copies and reached number five on the charts.

On January 26, 1955, "Davy Crockett Goes to Congress" was broadcast on the nation's small screens. "We filmed the Congress scenes at the Nashville, Tennessee, state house, and we actually used Andrew Jackson's home, The Hermitage, in the exterior shots," said Parker in a November 1987 interview in *The Alamo Journal,* the official publication of The Alamo Society.

On February 23, "Davy Crockett at the Alamo" aired. The episode's ending, which inspired a generation of youngsters around the nation to restage their own battle of the Alamo in backyards and city streets, is a classic. Crockett, depicted as the last defender, swings his rifle back and forth as Mexican soldiers climb the stairs and walls. Crockett is not shown dying; instead, the camera closes in on him as his inevitable fate approaches. "There was a concern by Disney to take into account both history and the feelings of the kids," said Parker in *The Alamo Journal* interview. "The final scene was definitely under-rehearsed. We had stunt men and stunt extras working in the scene, and there was a considerable amount of uncertain footing, especially where I was swinging my rifle back and forth." The ending's last shot is of the modern flag of Texas, which dissolves into the final page of Crockett's journal. Of all the Crockett and Alamo films, it is Fess Parker's image of Crockett swinging his rifle in a final act of supreme courage that remains most memorable of all. Disney repeated the three episodes on April 13, April 27, and May 11.

The April 25, 1955, issue of *Life* magazine chronicled the growing Davy Crockett Craze with a vivid seven-page spread. Life reported that "raccoon tails used to sell for 2-cents apiece, but with the shrill demand for coonskin hats, the market soared to 8-cents, and now it has become an open question which will be exhausted first: the supply of raccoons or the parents who have to buy the caps." However, the demand for coonskin caps became so great that raccoon tails increased in price to $5 each!

Davy Crockett merchandise filled the store shelves and the baby boomers purchased the items with glee. Disney marketed many items under the "Walt Disney's official Davy Crockett, King of the Wild Frontier," logo. In fact, Disney's agreement with various manufacturers left no doubt that his merchandise was not even to be associated with non-Disney, Crockett items. One contractual demand noted that certain display items were "for use only with the display and promotion of Davy Crockett (Fess Parker) Official Walt Disney designs, and products produced only by manufacturers authorized and licensed by Walt Disney Productions." Disney's numerous Crockett goods ranged from games, guitars, and pencil cases to puzzles, bubble gum cards, clothing and, of course, coonskin caps.

Disney kept up the Crockett interest by releasing an edited theatrical version of the three episodes for movie audiences in June of 1955. Fess Parker and Walt Disney appeared on the cover of *Look* magazine on July 26, 1955. In early August, Republic Pictures released *The Last Command,* an Alamo movie which starred Arthur Hunnicutt as a bearded and buckskinned Crockett. During the summer, Disney filmed new television episodes for the 1955-1956 season, which described events in Crockett's life before his fateful encounter at the Alamo. "Davy

Crockett's Keelboat Race" aired on November 16, 1955, and "Davy Crockett and the River Pirates" was broadcast on December 14, 1955. Both episodes, essentially the first "prequels" in television history, were repeated in January and February of 1956. And like the first three episodes, both were edited and released as a feature film.

Since Crockett was a historical character, he was marketed generically by hundreds of manufacturers. Thousands of objects were manufactured. Crockett curtains, rugs, lunch boxes, pinback buttons, glasses, cookies, plastic trains, lamps, furniture, rings, rubber knives, and toy guns flooded the market. *Time* magazine estimated that approximately $100,000,000 worth of Crockett merchandise was sold during the first quarter of 1955 alone. When the craze subsided in 1956, some $300,000,000 worth of items had been sold.

Amidst all of the toys and games during the Crockett Craze came James Shackford's excellent book *David Crockett: The Man and the Legend.* Shackford's superior work was augmented by dozens of other authors and publishers. Children's books in particular were popular, to say nothing of the various Davy Crockett comic books. Disney briefly revived interest in Crockett when he kicked off the 1958-1959 *Disneyland* television season with a rebroadcast of the original three episodes.

1960s

In 1960, John Wayne released his epic film, *The Alamo,* in which he starred as Davy Crockett. Wayne's Crockett was a larger-than-life character who was quick with his fists and respectful of the ladies. The next year, Anne Ford wrote the children's book *Davy Crockett: A See and Read Biography.* During the mid-sixties, additional songs were recorded about Crockett. Even Disney attempted a Crockett revival of sorts when the three episodes were rebroadcast to kick off the 1963-1964 television season's debut of *Walt Disney's Wonderful World of Color* on three consecutive weeks beginning September 8, 1963. In fact, Disney took out a full-page ad in *Billboard* magazine and heralded the Crockett craze of the previous decade. Stated the ad: "Remember? 1955.

Davy Crockett took the nation by storm. 10,000,000 single records were sold! 750,000 albums were sold!"

1970s

During the 1970s, the 1837 *Crockett Almanack* was reprinted by the Huntington Library and Art Gallery, Richard M. Dorson edited *Davy Crockett: American Comic Legend*, and Dee Hicks recorded the song "Davy Crockett." Davy Crockett even appeared in a 1971 episode of *You Are There*, a program which brought viewers back to the past. In 1975, Carmen Perry's translation of the José Enrique de la Peña papers stated that Crockett survived the Battle of the Alamo, was captured, and executed. Dan Kilgore's controversial 1978 book, *How Did Davy Die?*, supported Perry's allegation.

1980s

The 1980s saw another Crockett renaissance, since the decade marked the bicentennial of the famous frontiersman's birth in 1986. The year also marked the Texas Sesquicentennial. Celebrations were held at Crockett's birthplace in Tennessee and San Antonio, Texas. Disney produced a new Davy Crockett series for television, starring Tim Dunigan in the title role, and *Texas Monthly* featured a cover story titled "Davy Crockett, Still King of the Wild Frontier" by Paul Andrew Hutton. The magazine also featured an interview with Fess Parker. James Shackford's definitive biography, *David Crockett; The Man and the Legend*, was also reprinted in 1986 by the University of North Carolina Press. And Walt Disney's *Davy Crockett, King of the Wild Frontier*, was released on videocassette. The best book of the decade was *Crockett at Two Hundred; New Perspectives on the Man and the Myth*, which was carefully edited in 1989 by Michael A. Lofaro and Joe Cummings. Other notable books included Richard Boyd Hauck's *Crockett: A Bio-Bibliography*, and a University of Nebraska Press release of Crockett's 1834 autobiography, with a lively and informative introduction by Paul Andrew Hutton.

Crockett's image and the actors who portrayed him over the years appeared on a series of *Alamo Journal* covers beginning in 1987. The publication examined every facet of his legend.

1990s

In the 1990s more Crockett titles appeared than any other time except the 1950s. Bill Groneman countered Dan Gilgore and other de la Peña supporters with *Defense of a Legend;* Disney Press released a half-dozen new Crockett books for young readers; Mark Derr penned *The Frontiersman: The Real Life and the Many Legends of Davy Crockett,* and Paul Anderson chronicled *The Davy Crockett Craze.* Jeff Long trashed the "king of the wild frontier" in *Duel of Eagles,* Cameron Judd created a lusty fictionalized frontiersman in *Crockett of Tennessee,* and noted Civil War historian William C. Davis traced Crockett's life in 1998 with his comprehensive *Three Roads to the Alamo.* Western writer David Thompson wrote eight fictional tales about Crockett in 1997 and 1998. Bill Groneman explored the controversy of Crockett's final moments in the 1999 book *Death of a Legend.*

21st Century

The legend of Davy Crockett will continue as new authors, artists, and film makers add to the enormous body of popular culture that is "half-horse and half-alligator."

Davy Crockett lives!

DAVID CROCKETT CHRONOLOGY

"Davy Crockett as a Teenager" illustration by Mike Boldt

DAVID CROCKETT TIME LINE

1786   Birth of David Crockett on August 17 to John and Rebecca Crockett, in a cabin at the juncture of the Nolichucky River and Limestone Creek in Tennessee.

1788   Crockett's father briefly leaves him and his family to participate in a military expedition against the Chickamaugas.

1792   John Crockett moves his family to a 197-acre site on Stockton's Fort of Lick Creek in Tennessee.

1793   John Crockett sells his 197-acre tract to Thomas Ray. The Crocketts move to a site on Cove Creek in Green County where John Crockett and partner Thomas Galbreath build a gristmill.

1794   A flood destroys John Crockett's mill on Cove Creek. The Crocketts move to a rented home in Jefferson County.

1796   John Crockett opens a taven on the Knoxville-Abington Road. Tennessee joins the Union on June 1 as the sixteenth state.

1798   Young David Crockett works as a drover for Jacob Siler.

1799   Crockett runs away from home after being threatened by his father for missing school. He finds employment at various unskilled jobs.

1800   Crockett travels to Baltimore, Maryland, where he works as a teamster.

1802   Crockett returns home.

1803   Crockett works off two of his father's oustanding debts.

1805   Margaret Elder terminates her unceremonious engagement with Crockett.

1806   Crockett marries Mary (Polly) Finley at Finley's Gap on August 14, in Jefferson County, Tennessee.

1807   Polly Crockett gives birth to a son, John Wesley, on July 10.

1809   Polly Crockett gives birth to a second son, William, on November 25.

1811   Crockett and his family move to a site on Mulberry Creek in Lincoln County, Tennessee.

1812   Polly Crockett gives birth to a daughter, Margaret Finley, on November 25.

1813   Crockett and his family move to a site on Bean's Creek in Franklin County, Tennessee. Crockett volunteers to serve a ninety-day enlistment in the Creek Indian War. He participates in the Battle of Tallusahatchee before returning home in December.

1814   Crockett reenlists and joins in expeditions against the Indians in Spanish Florida. The Treaty of Ghent formally ends the War of 1812 on December 24.

1815   Sgt. David Crockett returns home at the end of his reenlistment. Polly dies at age twenty-seven.

1816   Franklin County's 32nd Militia regiment elects Crockett a lieutenant. He marries widow Elizabeth Patton. He explores the Alabama Territory, and battles a near death-like case of malaria. Elizabeth Patton Crockett gives birth to a son, Robert Patton, on September 16.

1817   Crockett and his family move to a site on Shoal Creek in Lawrence County, Tennessee. He is elected to a position of justice of the peace.

1818   Crockett is elected to the position of colonel in the Lawrence County-based 57th Regiment of Militia. He serves as town commissioner of Lawrenceburg. Elizabeth Patton Crockett gives birth to a daughter, Rebecca Elvira, on December 25.

1819   Crockett resigns the office of justice of the peace.

1820   Crockett expresses interest in running for elected office.

1821   Crockett resigns his town commissioner office. He is elected to the Tennessee state legislature in Nashville. Elizabeth Patton Crockett gives birth to a second daughter, Matilda, on August 2.

1823   Crockett is re-elected to the Tennessee state legislature.

1824   Crockett completes his term in the Tennessee state legislature. Andrew Jackson loses the presidential election to John Quincy Adams.

1825   Crockett is defeated in his bid for a seat in the United States House of Representatives by Col. Adam Alexander.

1826   Crockett survives a Mississippi River boat wreck.

1827   Crockett is elected to the United States House of Representatives in the 20th Congress.

1828   Andrew Jackson wins the presidential election.

1829   Crockett is reelected to the House of Representatives in the 21st Congress.

1830   Crockett voices his disapproval of the Jackson administration's Indian Resettlement Act.

1831   Crockett is defeated in his reelection bid. The James Kirke Paulding Play, *The Lion of the West,* which is based on Crockett's life, debuts.

1832   Andrew Jackson is reelected; Martin Van Buren becomes vice-president.

1833   Crockett is elected to the House of Representatives in the 23rd Congress. Matthew St. Clair Clarke's *Sketches and Eccentricities of Colonel David Crockett of West Tennessee* is published.

1834   *A Narrative of the Life of David Crockett of the State of Tennessee,* Crockett's autobiography, is published. Crockett conducts a political tour of the Northeast. He is presented a rifle, "Pretty Betsey," by the Young Whigs of Philadelphia. Several artists complete images of Crockett, including John Naegle and Anthony DeRose.

1835   Two ghostwritten Crockett books are published: *Col. Crockett's Tour to the North and Down East* and the *Life of Martin Van Buren.* The first Crockett almanac is published. *"Go Ahead," a march dedicated to Colonel Crockett* is published. Crockett is defeated in his reelection bid and departs Tennessee for Texas.

1836   Crockett travels to Texas and joins the forces opposed to the dictatorship of General Santa Anna. He participates in the Siege and Battle of the Alamo, where he dies on March 6, 1836. Some newspapers describe Crockett dy-

ing in battle, others state that he was captured and executed. Richard Penn Smith's *Col. Crockett's Exploits and
Adventures in Texas* is published.

1837   *Crockett's Free and Easy Songbook,* a popular stage song collection, is published. Crockett's eldest son, John Wesley
Crockett, is elected to Congress.

1838   The *Crockett Almanack, 1838,* features a reference to the
Alamo.

1839   *Colonel Crockett: A Virginia Reel* is published. John Wesley
Crockett is re-elected to Congress.

1845   Texas joins the Union as the twenty-eighth state.

1846   A new edition of *Crockett's Free and Easy Songbook* is published. William Crockett, David and Polly's second son,
dies on January 12.

1853   Clipper ship *David Crockett* is launched.

1854   John Wesley Crockett, David and Polly's first child, dies
on November 24.

1856   The final *Crockett Almanack* is published.

1860   Elizabeth Patton Crockett, David's second wife dies on
January 31.

1871   Crockett County in Tennessee, is formed.

1872   Frank Murdock and Frank Mayo's play, *Davy Crockett: Or,
Be Sure You're Right, Then Go Ahead,* debuts with Mayo in
the lead.

1877   *Davy Crockett: Or, Be Sure You're Right, Then Go Ahead,* is
performed for the one thousandth time.

1879   Rebecca Elvira Crockett, David and Elizabeth's first
daughter, dies on March 23.

1886   Kit Clyde's *Davy Crockett's Vow, or, His Last Shot for Vengeance,* is published.

1889   A limestone marker is dedicated at a recreated frontier
cabin, which designates Crockett's Tennessee birthplace.
Robert Patton, David and Elizabeth's first son, dies on
August 3.

1890   Matilda Crockett, David and Elizabeth's second daughter, dies on August 2.

1896   The play *Davy Crockett: Or, Be Sure You're Right, Then Go
Ahead,* closes upon the death of its lead performer, Frank
Mayo.

1905   Harriet G. Reiter's *David Crockett* is published as part of the Instructor Literature Series.

1908   Edward Willett's *Davy Crockett's Boy Hunter,* is published as part of the Beadles Frontier Series.

1909   Charles K. French stars in the first Crockett film, the silent one-reeler, *Davy Crockett - in Hearts United.*

1910   The silent film *Davy Crockett* is released.

1911   The silent film *The Immortal Alamo* is released featuring a saber-wielding Crockett.

1915   A. D. Sears stars as Crockett in the silent film *The Martyrs of the Alamo.*

1916   Dustin Farnum is featured in the title role of the silent film *Davy Crockett.*

1926   Cullen Landis stars as Crockett in the silent film *Davy Crockett at the Fall of the Alamo.*

1934   Constance Rourke's *Davy Crockett* is published.

1937   Lane Chandler stars as Crockett in *Heroes of the Alamo.*

1938   Sterling Waters stars as Crockett in *The Alamo, "Shrine of Texas Liberty."*

1939   Robert Barratt stars as Crockett in *Man of Conquest.*

1941   William "Wild Bill" Elliott stars in the film *The Son of Davy Crockett.*

1942   Dee Brown's *Wave High the Banner: A Novel Based on the Life of Davy Crockett* is published.

1950   George Montgomery has the title role in *Davy Crockett, Indian Scout.*

1951   *Frontier Fighter Davy Crockett,* first post-WWII Crockett comic book is published by Avon Comics.

1953   Trevor Bardette stars as Crockett in *Man From the Alamo.*

1954   "Davy Crockett, Indian Fighter," starring Fess Parker, debuts on Walt Disney's *Disneyland* TV show on December 15. "The Ballad of Davy Crockett" is recorded.

1955   "Davy Crockett Goes to Congress" is broadcast on *Disneyland* on January 26 (it is repeated on April 27). "Davy Crockett at the Alamo" is broadcast on February 23 (it is repeated on May 11). "Davy Crockett, Indian Fighter" is repeated on April 13. Disney edits the three episodes as a theatrical release, *Davy Crockett, King of the Wild Frontier.* Bill Hayes' version of "The Ballad of Davy Crockett" reaches Number one on the *Billboard* charts. "Davy

Crockett's Keelboat Race" is broadcast on November 16 and "Davy Crockett and the River Pirates" is broadcast on December 14. Arthur Hunnicutt stars as Davy Crockett in *The Last Command.*

1956   "Davy Crockett's Keelboat Race" is repeated on *Disneyland* on January 25. "Davy Crockett and the River Pirates" is repeated on on February 22. Both TV episodes are edited as a theatrical release, *Davy Crockett and the River Pirates.* James Griffith stars as Crockett in *The First Texan.* James A. Shackford's *David Crockett, The Man and the Legend* is published.

1959   Fess Parker appears briefly as Crockett in the comedy film *Alias Jesse James.*

1960   John Wayne stars as Crockett in *The Alamo.*

1963   Gold Key Comics reprints *Davy Crockett, King of the Wild Frontier.*

1967   U.S. Post Office issues a first-class five-cent stamp commemorating Davy Crockett.

1969   Gold Key Comics reprints *Davy Crockett, King of the Wild Frontier* for a second time.

1971   Fred Gwynne appears as Davy Crockett in a "Siege of the Alamo" episode on CBS-TV's *You Are There.*

1976   Crockett is featured as card number nine in the fifty-card "A Great American" trading card set during the Bicentennial.

1978   Dan Kilgore's *How Did Davy Die?* is published.

1982   Richard B. Houck's *Crockett: A Bio-Bibliography* is published.

1985   Michael A. Lofaro's *Davy Crockett: The Man, The Legend, The Legacy* is published.

1986   The bicenntennial of Crockett's birth is celebrated in Tennessee and Texas. The Alamo Society is created and Crockett is mentioned in the first issue of *The Alamo Journal,* the organization's official publication. "Crockett: Hero or Hype" is the November cover story of *Texas Monthly.*

1987   Brian Keith stars as Crockett in the TV movie *The Alamo: 13 Days to Glory.*

1988   Merrill Connally stars as Crockett in the IMAX film,

Alamo . . . the Price of Freedom. Tim Dunigan stars as Crockett in the new Disney TV episode "Rainbow in the Thunder."

1989 The essay collection *Crockett at Two Hundred* is published.

1991 Film director David Zucker makes a cameo appearance as Davy Crockett in *Naked Gun 2½: The Smell of Fear.*

1993 Mark Derr's *The Frontiersman: The Real Life and Many Legends of Davy Crockett* is published. Artist John Nava paints the canvas *David Crockett 1812.*

1994 Bill Groneman's *Defense of a Legend; Crockett and the de la Peña Diary* is published. Noel Webb appears as a holographic Davy Crockett in the San Antonio-located Texas Adventure.™

1995 John Schneider stars as Crockett in the two-part TV movie *James A. Michener's "Texas."* Artist Michel Schreck paints the canvas *Davy Crockett.*

1996 Paul F. Anderson's *The Davy Crockett Craze* is published.

1997 Artist Mark Churms paints *Davy Crockett's Last Sunrise.* David Thompson writes *Homecoming,* the first in his fictional series on Crockett.

1999 Bill Groneman's *Death of a Legend* is published. David Wright paints the canvas *Crossroads to Destiny.*

2000 *The Davy Crockett Almanac & Book of Lists* is published.

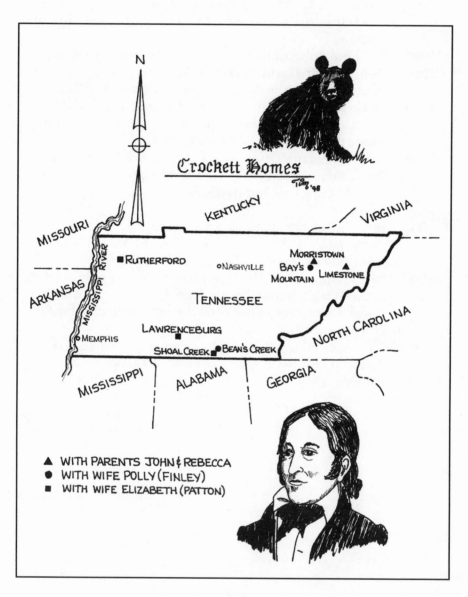

"Crockett homes" illustration by Rod Timanus.

DAVID CROCKETT FAMILY TREE

DAVID CROCKETT FAMILY TREE

David Crockett

Born: August 17, 1786
Died: March 6, 1836
Father: John Crockett
Mother: Rebecca Hawkins
Wife: Mary Polly Finley (1788-1815)
Children: John Wesley Crockett (July 10, 1807-
                November 24, 1854)
            William Crockett (November 25, 1809-
                January 12, 1846)
            Margaret Finley Crockett (November 25, 1812-
                before 1860)

Wife: Elizabeth Patton (May 22, 1788-January 31, 1860)
Children: Robert Patton Crockett (September 16, 1816-
                August 3, 1889)
            Rebecca Elvira Crockett (December 25, 1818-
                March 23, 1879)
            Matilda Crockett (August 2, 1821-July 6, 1890)

Crockett Grandchildren

Parents: John Wesley Crockett and Martha Turner
                Hamilton (1809-1873)
            Mary Elizabeth Crockett (1830-1873)
            Robert Hamilton Crockett (1838-1902)
            Alice Ann Crockett (1839-1886)
            Peytonia P. Crockett (1847-1897)

Charles Waters Crockett (1849-1920)
Susan Crockett (1852-1885)

Parents: William Crockett and Clorinda Boyett (1809-?)
David Crockett (1830-1870)
William A. Crockett (1839-1877)

Parents: Margaret Finley Crockett and Wiley Flowers
(1805-1868)
Mary Elvira Flowers (1831-?)
Harriet Flowers (1833-1890)
Martha Matilda Flowers (1835-?)
Maria Louisa Flowers (1838-?)
David Finley Flowers (1844-1924)
David [twin] Flowers (1844-?)
Sarah Ann Flowers (1847-?)
Mary Margaret Flowers (1853-?)
John Wesley Crockett Flowers (1854-?)

Parents: Robert Patton Crockett and Matilda Porter
(1823-1864)
Martha Melinda Crockett (1842-1914)
John Bell Crockett (1844-?)
William Henry Harrison Crockett (1846-?)
David Thomas Crockett (1848-1918)
Bolden Avery Crockett (1852-1904)
Mary Elizabeth Crockett (1855-?)
Ashley Wilson Crockett (1857-1954)
Dorcas Matilda Crockett (1860-1948)
Olivia Elvira Crockett (1863-1953)

Parents: Rebecca Elvira Crockett and George Kimbro
[Kimbrough]
Elizabeth A. Kimbrough (1839-?)
Martha Kimbrough (1842-?)
J. C. Kimbrough (1844-?)

Parents: Rebecca Elvira Crockett and [second husband]
James M. Halford (1816-1863)

Jefferson C. Halford (1847-?)
Robert C. Halford (1850-?)
William Graves Halford (1856-?)
J. B. Halford (1861-?)

Parents: Matilda Crockett and Thomas P. Tyson (?-1850)
             Mary Elizabeth Tyson (1838-1896)
             Candis Queen Tyson (1841-1918)

CROCKETT
FROM
"A" TO "Z"

Davy Crockett
at the End of
the Creek War.

"Davy Crockett at the End of the Creek War" illustration by Gary Zaboly.

A Narrative of the Life of David Crockett of the State of Tennessee
    David Crockett's autobiography published by E. L. Carey and A. Hart of Philadelphia in 1834. Edited by Thomas Chilton of Kentucky, *A Narrative of the Life of David Crockett of the State of Tennessee*, was a best-seller which promoted the Congressman's popularity throughout the United States. In fact, the book's publication coincided with Crockett's political tour of the northeastern states in 1834. The book has been constantly reprinted over the years.

A Narrative of the Life of David Crockett of the State of Tennessee
    Facsimile 1973 edition of Crockett's 1834 autobiography. The "Tennesseana" edition features an introduction and annotations by James A. Shackford and Stanley J. Folmsbee. The book was reprinted as a paperback in 1987 and 1995.

A Narrative of the Life of David Crockett of the State of Tennessee
    Joseph John Arpad's edited 1972 book about the famous nineteenth century frontier personality. *A Narrative of the Life of David Crockett of the State of Tennessee* was part of the "Masterworks of Literature Series."

Abbott, John S. C.
    Author of the 1874 book, *David Crockett: His Life and Adventures.*

Account of Colonel Crockett's Tour to the North and Down East, An
    Ghost-written, Whig-supported book published in 1835 which celebrated Crockett's 1834 tour of the Northeast.

Adeline
    Slave girl (also known as "Adaline") who was sold by Crockett in December of 1831 to help pay off a debt.

59

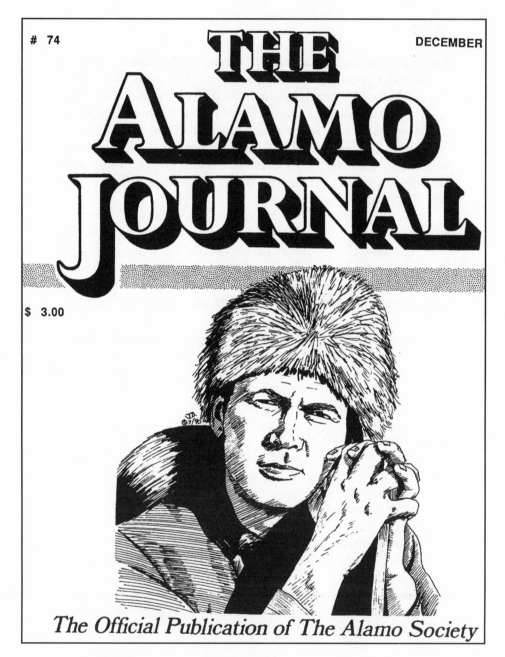

The Alamo Journal, *December 1990, illustration by John Bourdage.*

Adler, David A.
Author of the 1996 children's book, *A Picture Book of Davy Crockett.*

***Adventures of Davy Crockett, The;* Told Mostly by Himself**
Popular 1935 reprint which combines the 1834 *Narrative of the Life of David Crockett of the State of Tennessee* and Richard Penn's Smith's 1836 title, *Col. Crockett's Exploits and Adventures in Texas.*

Alamo Almanac & Book of Lists
William R. Chemerka's 1997 book about the Alamo of history and popular culture. The reference work features dozens of Alamo book titles that describe the various accounts of Crockett's death at the famous mission-fortress in 1836. *The Alamo Almanac & Book of Lists'* cover painting, *For God and Texas,* created by Richard Luce, depicts Crockett defending the Alamo palisade during the March 6, 1836, battle.

Alamo Journal, The
The official publication of The Alamo Society, which has featured scores of articles on David Crockett since its initial issue in 1986. Images of the Crockett of history and the Crockett of popular culture have graced many of the periodical's covers over the years as well. *The Alamo Journal* focused on the controversial death of Crockett in a series of lengthy articles written by Dr. James Crisp, associate professor of history at North Carolina State University, and Texas-based researcher Thomas Ricks Lindley in the 1990s.

Alexander, Col. Adam
One of two major candidates (General William Arnold was the other) who lost to Crockett in the 1827 House of Representatives election for Tennessee's Ninth Congressional District.

Alias Jesse James
Title of 1959 western comedy starring Bob Hope, which featured Fess Parker in a cameo role as Davy Crockett, the character he made famous in the 1954-1955 television series produced by Walt Disney.

All About Crockett

A 1995 Crockett County (Tennessee) Chamber of Commerce booklet that promotes such enterprises as the Bank of Crockett, the Crockett Mills Cotton Gin, and the Crockett Golf & Country Club.

Allen, Charles Fletcher

Author of the 1911 biography *David Crockett: Scout, Small Boy, Pilgrim, Mountaineer, Soldier, Bear-Hunter, and Congressman— Defender of the Alamo.*

Anderson, Paul F.

Author of the 1996 book *The Davy Crockett Craze: A Look at the 1950s Phenomenon and Davy Crockett Collectibles.* Anderson penned a comprehensive article on the Crockett craze in issue number five (1993) of his own Disney tribute quarterly, *Persistence of Vision.* The author called for a revival of the 1950s Davy Crockett craze as a tonic for modern society's moral malaise: "Come to think of it, with the seeming move away from the traditonal American values represented by Crockett—truth, honor, patriotism, virtue, duty, chivalry, sincerity—a good old Davy Crockett craze might just help!"

Arnold, Guy

Unbilled extra who portrayed the corpse of Davy Crockett in the Alamo aftermath scene of the 1986 television movie *Houston: The Legend of Texas* (video title: *Gone To Texas*).

Arnold, Gen. William

One of two major candidates (Col. Adam Alexander was the other) who lost to Crockett in the 1827 House of Representatives election for Tennessee's Ninth Congressional District.

Arpad, Joseph John

Editor of the 1972 book *A Narrative of the Life of David Crockett of the State of Tennessee.* Arpad's 1969 Ph.D. dissertation was titled "Davy Crockett, An Original Legendary Eccentricity and Early American Character."

Autobiography of David Crockett, The
Title in Scribner's "Modern Student's Library" series. Published in 1923, the autobiography features a noteworthy introduction by Hamlin Garland.

"Ballad of Davy Crockett, The"
Popular tune written by Tom Blackburn (lyrics) and George Bruns (music) that accompanied Walt Disney's *Davy Crockett, King of the Wild Frontier* during the 1954-1955 television season. The twenty-verse song published by Wonderland Music Company, was abbreviated by the several dozen artists who recorded it. Orchestra and choral leader Fred Waring recorded a complete version that logged in at nine minutes. Several other versions were chart successes, including Walter Schumann (#14), "Tennessee" Ernie Ford (#5), Fess Parker (#5) and Bill Hayes (#1), who topped the charts for five weeks. Other artists who recorded the Blackburn-Bruns composition included Gabe Drake and the Woodsman, Tex Ritter, Rusty Draper, Karen and Cubby, Tommy Scott, John Brown and the Trailwinders, the Sons of the Pioneers, Mac Wiseman, Jack Richards with the Corwin Group, Bill Ruff and the Four Jacks, Steve Allen, and Bill Hart and the Mountaineers, among additional performers. Peder Fess Gustawson, a Crockett researcher from Sweden, reviewed the three *Davy Crockett, King of the Wild Frontier* episodes, and concluded that the ballad actually contained twenty-nine verses (nine additional verses were created as transitional pieces integrated within scenes from the 1954-1955 television trilogy). The complete lyrics of "The Ballad of Davy Crockett" were printed in issue #76 (April 1991) of *The Alamo Journal.* In addition, a number of other artists released Crockett song parodies, including Irving Fields' "Davy Crockett Mambo," Stepin Fetchit's "Davy Crockett Boogie," Homer and Jethro's "The Ballad of Davy Crewcut," and Mel Blanc's "Woody Woodpecker Meets Davy Crockett."

Bardette, Trevor
Actor who played Davy Crockett in the 1953 motion picture, *The Man From the Alamo*.

Barratt, Robert
Actor who played Davy Crockett in the 1939 motion picture *Man of Conquest*. Barratt dropped one of the "T's" from his last name by the time he appeared as the Indian, Lone Eagle, in the 1950 film *Davy Crockett Indian Scout,* which starred George Montgomery.

Baugh, Virgil
Author of the 1960 book *Rendezvous at the Alamo: Highlights in the Lives of Bowie, Crockett & Travis.*

Beals, Frank
Author of the 1941 children's book, *Davy Crockett.*

Bearden, Jeff
Texas-based historical interpreter who has portrayed Crockett at numerous historical presentations since the Lone Star State Sesquicentennial in 1986. In addition, Bearden portrayed Crockett on the Discovery Channel's "Battle of the Alamo" episode in 1994, and the History Channel's special on "The Alamo" in 1995.

Becknell, William
Friend of Crockett whom the famous frontiersman visited for several days in Texas prior to the siege of the Alamo.

Beecher, Elizabeth
Author of the authorized 1955 book, *Walt Disney's Davy Crockett, King of the Wild Frontier.*

Bender, Howard
New Jersey-based illustrator and Crockett memorabilia collector who created a number of Crockett images for *The Alamo Journal*. His large collection of Crockett toys from the 1950s was featured on the television program *Collector's FX* in 1995. Bender also created and maintains the Internet website "Croktcraze," a nostalgic salute to Walt Disney's *Davy Crockett, King of the Wild Frontier.*

Ben Hardin's Crockett Almanac of 1842

Publication which featured the first illustration of Crockett battling at the Alamo. An unknown artist depicted Crockett with the caption "Crockett's Fight With The Mexicans." The almanac also promoted the idea that Crockett had been captured at the Alamo and sent to Mexico to work in the mines.

Benton, Thomas Hart

U.S. Senator from Missouri who declined a Whig Party offer in 1834 to run for vice president in 1836 against the Democrats. When Benton declined the offer and urged support for Martin Van Buren, Andrew Jackson's vice president, Crockett parodied the Congressman in a series of newspaper-published letters in 1835.

Benton, Thomas Hart

Noted twentieth century painter who was approached by Walt Disney in 1946 to create a cartoon operetta based on the life of Davy Crockett. According to a 1990 Los Angeles County Museum of Art exhibition guide book, Benton told the Disney studio that, "he found it impossible to create anything satisfying within the constraints the studio imposed." Disney waited until 1954 to revive his Crockett project: the epic television trilogy "Davy Crockett, King of the Wild Frontier."

Biddle, Nicholas

President of the Second Bank of the United States and Whig Party activist. On at least one occasion, Biddle granted Crockett, a fellow Whig, a loan, which he later forgave.

Big Clover Lick Creek

Site in Tennessee (actually the area of Big and Little Clover Lick Creeks) where Crockett killed three bears in one day during an autumn 1825 hunt.

Bigelow, Elijah

Publisher (with Col. Charles D. McClean) of the *Jackson Gazette* (formerly the *Jackson Pioneer*), a west Tennessee newspaper that supported Crockett politically in 1824 during the frontiersman's run for the state legislature.

"Billy Buckskin"

Fictional comic book character modeled on Davy Crockett during the mid-1950s. The *Billy Buckskin Western* comics even carried the Disney-like phrase "Tales of the Wild Frontier" on the cover. Furthermore, issue number three (in March of 1956) featured an ad by the Daisy Manufacturing Company, which offered "Walt Disney's official Davy Crockett charm."

Bishop, Lee

Author of the 1983 paperback, *Davy Crockett: Frontier Fighter.*

Blackburn, Tom

Scriptwriter who penned Walt Disney's *Davy Crockett, King of the Wild Frontier,* which aired during the 1954-1955 television season. Blackburn also wrote the lyrics to the popular "The Ballad of Davy Crockett" in 1954 and other related songs which appeared in the five episodes, including "King of the River" and "Yaller, Yaller Gold."

Blair, Walter

Author of the 1955 book, *Davy Crockett—Legendary Frontier Hero: The Truth as He Told It—The Legend as His Friends Built It.*

Blassingame, Wyatt

Author of the 1972 children's publication *How Davy Crockett Got A Bearskin Coat.*

Blood Hunt

David Thompson's third title in his fictional "Davy Crockett" series. Crockett's loyal friend Flavius Harris joins the famous pioneer in *Blood Hunt* on another frontier sojourn where they battle the Indians.

Blood Rage

One of David Thompson's paperback titles in his "Davy Crockett" series. In *Blood Rage* (1997), Crockett heads west to battle the Pawnees and saves a wagonload of settlers.

Bode, Robert

New York-based artist who created the 1967 five-cent Davy Crockett stamp for the United States Post Office.

Bowie Knife

Large hunting/butcher knife associated with James Bowie, who died with Crockett at the Alamo on March 6, 1836. A Bowie Knife on display in the Bedford, Massachusetts, Public Library in 1990 was allegedly given to Davy Crockett by Bowie. The knife's blade is allegedly signed by Crockett as "Crocket." Crockett portrait artist John Chapman noticed the famous frontiersman carrying a "large knife . . . which is inscribed 'Crocket.'"

Brown, Dee

Author of the 1942 book *Wave High The Banner: A Novel based on the Life of Davy Crockett.*

Burke, James Wakefield

Author of the 1984 book *David Crockett, The Man Behind the Myth.*

Burton, Ardis Edwards

Author of the authorized 1955 Walt Disney children's book, *Legends of Davy Crockett*

Butler, William E.

Candidate who Crockett defeated in the 1823 Tennessee state legislature election.

Cage, Nicholas

Actor who narrated the 1992 children's audiocassette, *Davy Crockett.*

Camden, New Jersey

Site of May 1834 pickpocketing of Crockett. A sum of $186 was stolen from Crockett who suggested that "it must be a Jackson man who did it." In July of 1834, Crockett crossed the Delaware River from Philadelphia to Camden to fire the rifle given to him by the Young Whigs of Philadelphia.

Camden and Amboy Railroad

New Jersey-based railroad which Crockett used during the spring of 1834 during his Whig-promoted tour of the Northeast United States.

Canady, John Jr.

Quaker friend/father figure of David Crockett when the famous Tennessean was in his teens. According to Joseph A. Swann, author of the unpublished manuscript, *The Early Life & Times of David Crockett:* "The influence of John Canady on David was profound. John Canady became the father model which David never had in his natural father."

Cannibal Country

One of David Thompson's paperback titles in his "Davy Crockett" series. In *Cannibal Country* (1998), Crockett meets up with Jim Bowie near the Gulf of Mexico where the two frontier legends battle cannibals.

Cash, Johnny

Legendary country singer who portrayed Crockett in 1988 sequences of "Rainbow in the Thunder," part of the new Davy Crockett series on *The Magical World of Disney.* Cash, portraying an older Crockett, is seen reminiscing with President Andrew Jackson before the episode flashes back to the Creek Indian War with a younger Crockett played by Tim Dunigan.

Cattermole, E. G.

Author of the late nineteenth century book, *Famous Frontiersmen, Pioneers, and Scouts: The Vanguards of American Civilization,* in which Crockett is included.

Chadwicke, Alice

Author of the 1956 play *Davy Crockett: A Robust Comedy Drama in Three Acts Based on the Life of America's Heroic Young Backwoodsman.*

Chandler, Lane

Actor who played Davy Crockett in the 1937 motion picture *Heroes of the Alamo.*

Chanticleer of the Wilderness Road: the Story of Davy Crockett

Meridel Le Sueur's 1951 children's book. Of Crockett's death: "There came the moment when all that was Davy

Crockett, made from the earth, from the flesh of others, his tall, spired brain, his panther heart of imagination, fell down, and all at the Alamo were lost in that final and lonely place."

Chapman, John G.
Nineteenth century artist who painted *David Crockett*, a full-size portrait in 1834. Chapman said of the famous frontiersman-Congressman: "Col. Crockett's command of verbal expression was very remarkable, say what he might, his meaning could never be misrepresented. He expressed opinions, and told stories, with unhesitating clearness of diction, often embellished with graphic touches of original wit and humor, sparkling, and even starling, yet never out of place or obtrusively ostentatious."

Chilton, Thomas
Kentucky member of the U.S. House of Representatives, and friend of the famous pioneer who edited Crockett's manuscript *A Narrative of the Life of Col. David Crockett of Tennessee*, which was published in 1834.

Churms, Mark
British artist who created the 1997 painting *Crockett's Last Sunrise*.

Clark, William
Probable author of *An Account of Colonel Crockett's Tour to the North and Down East* in 1834.

Clarke, Matthew St. Clair
Author of the 1833 biography *The Life and Adventures of Colonel David Crockett of West Tennessee*.

Clay, Edward
Nineteenth-century lithographic artist (born in 1799) who created the early 1830s image of Colonel Nimrod Wildfire, the Crockett-like stage character portrayed by James Hackett in James K. Paulding's play *The Lion of the West*. A waist-high version of this image graced the cover of *Davy Crockett's Almanack of Wild Sports in the West* in 1837.

Clayton, Augustin Smith
The probable author of Crockett's ghost-written *The Life of Martin Van Buren* in 1835.

Clyde, Kit
Author of the 1886 "dime novel" *Davy Crockett's Vow, or, His Last Shot for Vengeance.*

Coatsworth, Elizabeth Jane
Author of the 1953 children's book *Old Whirlwind: A Story of Davy Crockett.*

Cody, William F.
Author of the 1888 publication, *Story of the Wild West and Camp-Fire Chats, by Buffalo Bill, (Hon. William F. Cody): A Full and Complete History of the Renowned Pioneer Quartette, Boone, Crockett, Carson and Buffalo Bill.*

Cohen, Caron Lee
Author of the 1985 children's book *Sally Ann Thunder Ann Whirlwind Crockett.*

Col. Crockett's Co-operative Christmas
Rupert Hughes' 1906 book about Col. D. A. Crockett of Waco, Texas, and a Christmas dinner at Madison Square Garden.

Col. Crockett's Exploits and Adventures in Texas . . .
Written by Himself
Richard Penn Smith's 1836 book celebrating Crockett's participation in the Texas Revolution. Smith created a fictional entry in Crockett's "manuscript" for March 5, 1836, the day before he died at the Alamo: "Pop, pop, pop! Bom, bom, bom! throughout the day. No time for memorandum now. Go ahead! Liberty and independence forever!" Part of this conclusion was used as a graphic in the final scenes of Walt Disney's "Davy Crockett at the Alamo."

Col. Crockett, the Bear King
Edward S. Ellis' 1886 "dime novel" published under the name Charles E. LaSalle.

Col. David Crockett, the Celebrated Hunter, Wit, and Patriot
Title of 1861 Beadle's Dime Biographical Library booklet about Crockett, in which the famous frontiersman is identified as one of six Alamo defenders who survive the battle only to be subsequently executed. Of Crockett's death: "He died without a groan, 'a frown on his brow and a smile of scorn and defiance on his lips." The New York and London, England-produced publication added: "Had all the garrison fought with such an effort as David Crockett, that the band of one hundred and eighty-two Texans would have annihilated four thousand Mexicans!"

Comanche Country
One of David Thompson's paperback titles in his "Davy Crockett" series. In *Comanche Country* (1998), Crockett and his sidekick, Flavius Harris, sojourn west of the Mississippi to tangle with the Comanches.

Confessions of David Crockett, The
Steve Warren-penned play which was produced at the Hyde Park Theatre in Austin, Texas, in 1996. Crockett was played by Ernie Taliaferro.

Connally, Merrill
Actor who played David Crockett in the 1988 IMAX film *Alamo . . . The Price of Freedom.*

Constable, Richard
Philadelphia, Pennsylvania-based gunsmith who was commissioned by the Youngs Whigs of Philadelphia to build a rifle for Crockett in 1834.

Coon 'N Crockett MuzzleLoaders Club
Grand Forks, North Dakota-based organization formed in 1969 and chartered in 1973. The non-profit National Muzzleloading Rifle Association-chartered group is named after Crockett but was actually inspired by the 1972 film *Jeremiah Johnson.*

Corby, Jane
Author of the 1922 children's book *The Story of Davy Crockett*.

Cowan, John
Captain of Crockett's company during War of 1812 enlistment period of September 28, 1814, to March 27, 1815.

Crockett
East Texas town (1990 population: 7,315) named after the famous Alamo defender. Crockett, the seat of Houston County, features the Davy Crockett Memorial Park, the nearby Davy Crockett National Forest, and the Davy Crockett Spring. The Davy Crockett Memorial Park has been the site for the "Davy Crockett Pioneer Festival."

Crockett
Post office site created on December 12, 1829, in Gibson County, Tennessee, which Crockett gave as his official congressional home address during two of his two-year terms, which began in 1829 and 1833.

Crockett: a Bio-bibliography
Richard Boyd Hauck's informative 1982 narrative-reference book. The author provides separate narratives on Crockett's life and the history of the legendary frontiersman.

Crockett Adjustments
Little Rock, Arkansas-based property and casualty adjusting firm. The enterprise was founded in 1975 and is headed by Davy Crockett, a sixth-generation grandson of the famous frontiersman.

Crockett at Two Hundred
Collection of essays (complete title: *Crockett at Two Hundred: New Perspectives on the Man and the Myth*) edited by Michael A. Lofaro and Joe Cummings in 1989, which resulted from a 1986 symposium held on the campus of East Tennessee State University in Johnson City, Tennessee. The book contains such inter-

esting essays as "Crockett and Nineteenth-Century Music" (written by Charles K. Wolfe), and "Davy Crockett and the Tradition of the Westerner in American Cinema" (written by William Eric Jamborsky), among others. Contributor Miles Tanenbaum's excellent bibliography includes important primary and secondary sources, plus a roster of "Works Dealing With The Alamo and Texas Independence."

Crockett Cigars

Name of one of six Alamo Handmades, a "first-quality" cigar line currently sold by the Finck Cigar Company of San Antonio, Texas. The Crockett, which measures seven-inches in length, is made from Cuban seeds in Honduras. Other Alamo Handmades include the Esparza, Bowie, Stockton, Bonham, and Travis.

Crockett County (Tennessee)

West Tennessee county named after the famous frontiersman in 1871. The county seat, Alamo, is named after the famous mission-fortress where Crockett died on March 6, 1836. Over the years, the county featured such establishments as the Crockett Medical Clinic, the Crockett Memorial Library, and the Crockett Farmers Co-op.

Crockett County (Texas)

West central Texas county, which features the Crockett County Memorial Park, the Crockett County Museum, and the Davy Crockett Monument.

Crockett for Congress!

Unsuccessful 1996 Tennessee Republican primary congressional campaign waged by David Crockett (no relation to the famous David Crockett), then a district attorney from Washington County. Crockett was one of only six candidates who received more than 10,000 votes (actually 10,263) in the primary, but he finished sixth out of eleven in the field. Opponent Bill Jenkins not only won the primary, but won the general election to be the representative for Tennessee's First Congressional District in the House of Representatives. After the primary election, Crockett's campaign signs became collectors items.

Crockett: the Gentleman from the Cane

Gary L. Foreman's 1986 glossy booklet (complete title: *Crockett: The Gentleman from the Cane; A Comprehensive View of the Folkhero Americans Thought They Knew*) about the famous frontiersman's life in both history and popular culture. The author's excellent visual survey includes an original painting, *Davy and the Bear,* created by artist Eric Von Schmidt.

Crockett Hotel

San Antonio, Texas, facility located directly across the street from the Alamo Complex's southeastern corner. The 204-room hotel (a main building, constructed in 1909, and a separate motel-like wing) is listed on the National Register of Historic Structures. The Crockett Hotel has hosted meetings of the Direct Descendants of David Crockett and the Alamo Society.

Crockett for Judge!

Successful 1955 vote for Judge of Elections in Pittsburgh, Pennsylvania, won by the historical Davy Crockett via a write-in campaign! Crockett won the 7th District of the 6th Ward by one vote!

Crockett of Tennessee

Cameron Judd's 1994 fictional historical novel (complete title: *Crockett of Tennessee: A Novel Based on the Life and Times of David Crockett*). Of Crockett's death after his capture at the Alamo: "David, pierced again and again by bayonets, taking the assault without an outcry, claimed by his destiny, going to his glory-time like the bravest of soldiers."

Crockett Tavern

Boyhood "home" of David Crockett located in Morristown, Tennessee. The original structure, which was opened in 1796, was located some twelve miles north of Dandridge, Tennessee. According to Tim McCurry, who worked at the site for years, the original building was burned down in 1865 to curb the spread of smallpox. The recreated Morristown tavern was built in 1954 from original logs from pioneer homes of the period. The structure is filled with period items, some dating to 1785. An histor-

Davy Crockett at the Alamo illustration by Howard Bender.

ical marker outside the tavern states: "Here stood the Crockett Tavern, established and operated by John and Rebecca Crockett. It was the boyhood home of David Crockett (1786-1836), pioneer, political leader in Tennessee, and a victim of the Alamo Massacre at San Antonio, Texas." The Crockett Tavern received repair funds from the Association for the Preservation of Tennessee Antiquities during the early 1990s.

Crockett's Chocolate Raspberry
Gourmet coffee flavor in the "Texas Hero" line produced in the 1990s by the Cianfrani Coffee Company in Georgetown, Texas.

Crockett's Free-and-Easy Song Book
An 1837 collection (complete title: *Crockett's Free-And-Easy Song Book: A New Collection of the Most Popular Stage Songs, as Given By the Best Vocalists of the Present Day: and also of Favorite Dinner and Parlour Songs*) of contemporary tunes.

Crockett's Free-and-Easy Songbook
An 1846 collection (complete title: *Crockett's Free-and-Easy Songbook: Comic, Sentimental, Amatory, Sporting, African, Scotch, Irish, Western and Texian National, Military, Naval and Anacreonic: A New Collection of the Most Popular Stage Songs, Together with Glees, Duets, Recitations, and Medleys*) of contemporary tunes.

"Crockett's Last Stand"
Title of the highly-detailed diorama created in 1995 by Thomas F. Feely, Jr. for The Texas Adventure™ in San Antonio, Texas. "Crockett's Last Stand" features hundreds of one-of-kind figures, "exploding" artillery pieces, a synchronized audio track with music by Michael Boldt and narration by William R. Chemerka. Feely's diorama includes the Alamo church, the front courtyard, the palisade, the horse and cattle corrals, and the southern corner of the Long Barracks. The battling figure of Davy Crockett is the diorama's centerpiece. The diorama was displayed at The Texas Adventure™ from 1995 to 1999.

Crockett's Last Stand—A Diorama
Thomas F. Feely, Jr. and Nancy E. Nagle's 1995 booklet

which accompanied the debut of the diorama, "Crockett's Last Stand" at The Texas Adventure™ in San Antonio, Texas.

Crockett's Last Sunrise

Mark Churms' 1997 painting which depicts Crockett loading his rifle at the palisade during the Battle of the Alamo on March 6, 1836.

Crockett's Tavern

Restaurant-bar located at DisneyWorld's Fort Wilderness Resort in Orlando, Florida. The tavern's menu serves such items as the "Crockett's BBQ Sandwich," "Davy's Lemonade," and a number of alcoholic "Crockett's Frozen Specialities."

CROKTCRAZE@AOL.COM

The world wide web's premier site dedicated to the "King of the Wild Frontier." The site, which was created and developed by illustrator and Crockett collector Howard Bender, is located on the web at http://www.geocities.com/TelevisionCity/Set/1486/

Crossroads to Destiny

David Wright's 1999 painting which depicts Crockett, Andrew Jackson, Sam Houston, and Dr. Charles McKinney in 1813 at Camp Blount in Tennessee, during the Creek Indian War.

Daring Davy, The Young Bear Killer, or The Trail of the Border Wolf

Harry St. George's 1879 "dime novel" about Crockett's fictitious hunting exploits as a young man.

"Davey Crocked"

Name of comical brand of honey (full name of product: "Davey Crocked Blinded Tennessee Hydrated Bear Grease") produced in the 1980s by the Tropical Blossom Honey Company in Edgewater, Florida. The label features a picture of a tipsy Davy Crockett wearing a tilted coonskin cap.

David Crockett

Clipper ship named after the famous frontiersman. Built in the early 1850s and launched on October 18, 1853, the *David*

Crockett was built by the George Greenman Company in Connecticut for Handy & Everett of New York. The ship cost $94,800 and weighed 1,679 tons, which made it the heaviest craft constructed on the Mystic River. The *David Crockett* was a profitable ship for nearly forty years, primarily sailing the New York-to-San Francisco route after running the New York-to-Liverpool, Great Britain routes for a couple of years. The ship featured a life-size wooden figurehead of the famous frontiersman, but it was never mounted on the bow; instead, it was carried on board the three-masted vessel. In 1890, the *David Crockett* was unceremoniously converted to a barge by Peter Wright & Son of Philadelphia. The ship's final service was for Pocahontas Coal in New York City harbor. For nearly a decade, the once glorious ship served steam-powered vessels with its supplies of coal shipped in from Pennsylvania. The coal hulk was abandoned and left to decay in New York Bay in 1899. The floating remains of the *David Crockett*, with its masts still intact, were photographed at the turn of the twentieth century and included in Jane Lyon's 1962 book, *Clipper Ships and Captains,* which was part of the American Heritage Junior Library series. The beautiful figurehead of the ship was preserved and is currently displayed at San Francisco's Maritime Museum.

David Crockett

Harriet G. Reither's 1905 pamphlet that was part (#84) of the "Instructor Literature Series." The author traces Crockett's life from his childhood to the Alamo where he is one of six defenders who are captured at the end of the battle. Of Crockett's death: "But before [Crockett] reached [Santa Anna], a dozen bullets found their way in his heart."

David Crockett

Title of William Henry Huddle's nineteenth century painting of the famous frontier legend. The painting is currently held in the Archives Division of the Texas State Library.

David Crockett

Title of George Cary Eggleston's 1875 biography.

David Crockett: Backwoodsman and Congressman

Title of 1928 biographical pamphlet published by the John

Hancock Mutual Life Insurance Company of Boston, Massachusetts. The eighteen-page pamphlet was distributed freely by the
company. Of Crockett's death: "We do not know exactly how
Davy Crockett died. Some think that he was among the last six
survivors, that they surrendered and were taken before Santa
Anna, who ordered that they be killed at once. But it is more
probable that the brave woodsman died with his face to the foe,
undaunted and resolute,—on his lips, the words—'Go Ahead.'"
The company revised and expanded the pamphlet during the
Davy Crockett craze of 1955.

David Crockett: The Bravest of Them All Who Died in the Alamo
Vincent Frank Taylor's 1955 children's book which traces
Crockett's life retroactively. Of Crockett's death: "But there were
too many aiming muskets now, too many bayonets coming clos-
er. They shot him, and then they stabbed his lifeless body dozens
of times."

David Crockett 1812
Artist John Nava's 1993 painting of a young David Crockett
standing with rifle in hands on the eve of the Creek Indian War.
The painting is owned by David Zucker.

David Crockett: His Life and Adventures
John S. C. Abbott's 1874 biography. The author highlights
the "peculiar character" of Crockett from his childhood to his
participation in the siege and Battle of the Alamo in 1836. The
author noted that "Davy Crockett was not a model man. But he
was a representative man." Of Crockett's death after his capture,
Abbott stated: "Crockett, entirely unarmed, sprang, like a tiger,
at the throat of Santa Anna. But before he could reach him, a
dozen swords were sheathed in his heart, and he fell without a
word or a groan."

David Crockett—Scout
Frank McKernan's 1911 book about the renowned frontiersman.

David Crockett: Scout, Small Boy, Pilgrim, Mountaineer,
Soldier, Bear-Hunter, and Congressman—Defender of the Alamo
Charles Fletcher Allen's 1911 book. Of Crockett's death: "Like most of his companions, he died in his tracks, disdaining to ask for quarter."

David Crockett—Sure He Was Right
Mary Dodson Wade's 1992 children's book, in which Crockett's life is phrased in poetic-like stanzas. The book features dozens of illustrations by Pat Finney and a one-page glossary.

David Crockett, The Man and The Legend
James Akins Shackford's well-regarded, comprehensive 1956 scholarly biography. Shackford devotes considerable space to Crockett's political years and his legacy. The author provides details to the various descriptions of his death, but does not suggest the circumstances of Crockett's ultimate demise. Instead, the author states: "Too much has been made over the details of how David died at the Alamo. Such details are not important. What is important is that he died as he had lived. His life was one of idomitable bravery; his death was a death of intrepid courage."

David Crockett, The Man Behind the Myth
James Wakefield Burke's 1984 biography. Burke interjects fictional dialogue and contemporary commentary into this lively story of Crockett's life. Of Crockett's death after his capture: "Crockett feels absolutely no pain as the bayonets, swords and knives cut, slash, and hack his body to pieces."

Davis, Hazel
Author of the 1955 children's book *Davy Crockett: Frontiersman and Scout.*

Davis, James D.
Teenage Tennessean who described Crockett's clothing at the Union Hotel in Memphis on November 1, 1835: "[Crockett] wore that same veritable coon-skin cap and hunting shirt, bear-

ing upon his shoulder his ever faithful rifle." Crockett departed Memphis the next day for Texas.

Davis, William C.
Author of the 1998 book *Three Roads to the Alamo,* which traces the lives of Crockett, James Bowie, and William B. Travis.

Davy Crockett
Name of 1833 British-made steam locomotive that carried freight and passengers on the Saratoga and Schenectady Railroad in New York state. Designed by John B. Jervis and built by Robert Stephenson in April 1833 the *Davy Crockett* was a 4-2-0 style locomotive.

Davy Crockett
William C. Sprague's 1915 biography of the famous pioneer.

Davy Crockett
Constance Rourke's 1934 book which features an epilogue-bibliography of sorts, "Sunrise in His Pocket" and "Behind This Book." These concluding sections include a descriptive roster of *Davy Crockett Almanacs.* Of Crockett's death: "Crockett fell in the thickest of the swift and desperate clash [at the] wall on the south side toward the barracks."

Davy Crockett
Frank L. Beals' 1941 children's book. Reprinted in 1960, the book includes a series of questions relating to the text and other subjects, including civics, science, and ethics. Of Crockett's death: "Davy stood there alone, Old Betsy in hand. 'Liberty and Independence,' Davy called in a ringing voice. 'Go ahead, Texas! Go ahead, America!' Then slowly he slumped over the bodies of dead Mexicans."

"Davy Crockett"
Title of a number of independent and commercial recordings made prior to the enormously popular "Ballad of Davy Crockett" in 1954. Among the different songs that carried the title "Davy Crockett," were versions perfomed by Chubby Parker

(1931), Mrs. Minnie Floyd (1937), Lester Wells (1938), Mrs. Poromola Eddy (1938), Worthy Perkins (1939), Elmer Barton (1939), Pearl Brewer (1941), and Mrs. Will Redden (1941).

Davy Crockett
Title of 1955 biographical pamphlet published by the John Hancock Mutual Life Insurance Company of Boston, Massachusetts. The twenty-four-page pamphlet, which was distributed freely by the company, resembled a similar publication, *David Crockett: Backwoodsman and Congressman,* that was printed in 1928. Of Crockett's death: "Davy Crockett's body was found in the western corner among a heap of dead who looked like the very last stand of the Alamo."

Davy Crockett
Title of 1963 record album in United Artists' "Tale Spinners For Children" series. The long-playing disc features Denise Bryer and the Famous Theatre Company with the Hollywood Studio Orchestra.

Davy Crockett
Academic Industries' 1984 paperback for young readers. The Connecticut-based company's book tells Crockett's life in less than thirty pages, although several additional pages are devoted to review questions. Of Crockett's death: "Davy and the other men fought with guns, knives, and fists until not a man among them was still alive."

Davy Crockett
Felicity Trotman and Shirley Greenway's 1986 children's book. Illustrated by Chris Molan, the prose of *Davy Crockett* is arranged in a kind of poetic framework that is free of rhyme. Of Crockett's death: "Davy was killed where he stood, one of the last defenders of the Alamo."

Davy Crockett
Elliot Dooley's 1991 children's hard-bound comic book. The author's text traces Crockett's life from his youth to his final days at the Alamo. Of Crockett's death: "Hit savagely on the

back of the head, Davy Crockett fell to the ground, fatally wounded."

Davy Crockett

James Howard Kunstler's 1992 audiocassette story. Narrated by actor Nicholas Cage and featuring the music of David Bromberg, *Davy Crockett* is part of Rabbit Ears Productions' "American Heroes and Legends" series for children.

Davy Crockett, Jr., or "Be Sure You're Right, Then Go Ahead"

"Old Scout" 1905 "dime novel" in the Pluck and Luck series.

Davy Crockett Album

An undated British book (L. Miller and Son Ltd.) with no author cited. Augmented with comic strip panel art, the book features several stories including "Davy Crockett in Jamie and Cherokee Outwit the Creeks."

Davy Crockett: A Robust Comedy Drama in Three Acts Based on the Life of America's Heroic Young Backwoodsman

Alice Chadwick's 1956 play.

Davy Crockett: American Comic Legend

Richard M. Dorson's edited 1939 book of passages from the Crockett almanacs. Dorson's selections from the annual publications, which were printed from 1835 to 1856, are organized into the following categories: "The Legend Full-Blown," "Ring-Tailed Roarers," "Doughty Dames," "Ben Harding," "Davy Conquering Man," "Davy Conquering Beast," "Pedlars and Pukes," and "Davy in Lighter Moments." The editor also included many of the original almanac's lively graphics in the book.

"Davy Crockett: American Frontier Legend"

Arts & Entertainment network's 1994 episode in the cable television's network "Biography" series. The half-hour episode, which traced Crockett's life and legend from his birth in Tennessee to the Walt Disney-inspired Crockett craze of the mid-1950s, featured commentary by James Claborn, Gary Foreman, Paul Hutton, Michael Lofaro, and David Zucker.

Davy Crockett: American Hero

Bruce Grant's 1955 children's book. Illustrated by William Timmins, this informative Rand McNally "Elf" book provides details about flintlock rifle shooting in the pages devoted to Crockett's youth. Of Crockett's death: "No one, not even Davy Crockett, came out of the battle of the Alamo alive."

Davy Crockett: An American Hero

Tom Townsend's 1987 children's book which tells Crockett's story as a recollection from the Alamo in 1836. Of Crockett's death following his capture: "The one they called Crockett was coming towards [Santa Anna], a Bowie knife clutched in his left hand and death in his eyes. Santa Anna stepped backward as a dozen muskets fired around him."

Davy Crockett: A See and Read Biography

Anne Ford's 1961 children's book about the celebrated frontier hero.

Davy Crockett and His Coonskin Cap

Margery Evernden-penned children's play performed at the Casa Manana Playhouse in Fort Worth, Texas, on April 12, 13, 19, and 20, 1991.

Davy Crockett and Other Western Favorites

Happy Times Records' 1963 children's LP which featured "Davy Crockett" and the "Davy Crockett Pioneer March" along with eleven other sing-along traditional songs.

Davy Crockett and the Creek Indians

Justine Korman's 1991 children's book in the Disney "American Frontier" series about the Creek Indian War of 1813-1814.

Davy Crockett and the Highwaymen

Ron Fontes and Justine Korman's 1992 children's book in the Disney "American Frontier" series about Crockett's conflict with a group of claim jumpers. The story is based upon Crockett's battle with the character Big Foot Mason from "Davy Crockett Goes to Congress," the second episode in the 1954-1955 *Davy Crockett, King of the Wild Frontier* television trilogy.

Davy Crockett and the Indian Secret
James Duncan Lawrence's 1955 children's book. In this fictional tale, Crockett discovers the Indian secret: a treasure chest in a cave.

Davy Crockett and the Indians
Janet Frank's 1955 children's book, which was also published under the title *Straight-shootin' Davy.*

Davy Crockett and The King of the River
A. L. Singer's 1991 children's book in the Disney "American Frontier" series. The book is based upon the 1955 television episode "Davy Crockett's Keelboat Race."

Davy Crockett and Others in Fentress County Who Have Given the Country a Prominent Place in History
Albert Ross Hogue's 1955 book about the famous Tennessean. The author traces Crockett's life from his birth to his final days in Texas at the Alamo.

Davy Crockett and The Pirates at Cave-In Rock
A. L. Singer's 1991 children's book in the Disney "American Frontier" series. The book is based upon the 1955 television season episode "Davy Crockett and the River Pirates."

Davy Crockett and the River Pirates
Fifth and final episode in the five-episode *Davy Crockett, King of the Wild Frontier* 1954-1955 television series. Originally broadcast on December 14, 1955, the episode traces Crockett and Mike Fink's fight against the river pirates.

Davy Crockett and The River Pirates
Title of 1956 motion picture starring Fess Parker and Buddy Ebsen. The film was actually an edited version of two television episodes: "Davy Crockett's Keelboat Race" and "Davy Crockett and the River Pirates."

Davy Crockett and The River Pirates
Dell Comic book (#671) based on the Disneyland televsion episode "Davy Crockett and the River Pirates."

"Original home of David Crockett as it looked in 1932,
Gibson County, Tennessee."
— Photo courtesy of The Daughters of the Republic of
Texas Library at the Alamo

Davy Crockett at The Alamo

Justin Korman's 1991 children's book in the Disney "American Frontier" series. The author does not detail Crockett's death; instead, Korman stated: "[Crockett] and the others would defend the Alamo to the bitter end."

"Davy Crockett at The Alamo"

The third episode of the popular Walt Disney 1954-1955 television trilogy. The episode, which aired on February 23, 1955, and starred Fess Parker in the title role, traces Crockett's journey across the Mississippi River into Texas where he eventually travels to the Alamo. More than any other episode in the series, this one defined the character of Crockett for a generation of children. In the final scene, Parker is seen as the lone defender as Mexican infantrymen advance against him. His rifle empty, Parker ferociously swings "Old Betsy" back and forth. Several *soldados* fall, but others continue to advance. The camera, however, never reveals how Crockett perishes because it quickly shifts to a shot of the modern state flag of Texas. As the final page of Crockett's "Journal" is broadcast, the last lyrical line of "The Ballad of Davy Crockett" is performed in the background: "The storybooks tell they were all cut low/But the truth of it is this jest ain't so/For their spirits'll live an' their legends grow'/As long as we remember the Alamo/Davy, Davy Crockett. . . ."

Davy Crockett at The Alamo

Dell Comic book (#639) based on the 1955 *Disneyland* televison episode "Davy Crockett at the Alamo."

Davy Crockett Birthplace State Historical Area

Limestone, Tennessee, historic site which features a reproduction cabin and a Visitor's Center-Museum. In addition, the Davy Crockett Birthplace State Historical Area features a seventy-three-acre campground, three large picnic pavilions, and many scenic picnic areas. In 1973, the Davy Crockett Birthplace Association built a replica log cabin similar to the one Crockett was born in. Situated near the cabin is the Limestone Ruritan Club's monument to Davy Crockett. It features an open circular wall of stones which are native to the fifty states. On August 15-17, 1986, the site hosted a Davy Crockett Bicentennial Celebration. The site has also been on the itineray of select gatherings of the Direct Descendants of David Crockett.

Davy Crockett, Big Indian, and Little Bear
Harriet Evatt's 1955 children's book.

Davy Crockett: Danger From the Mountain
Nat Wilson's 1955 children's "Triple Nickel Book" about Crockett's fictitious exploits with the Crow Indians.

Davy Crockett/Daniel Boone
Naunerle C. Farr's 1979 dual biography for young readers. With comic panel art created by Fred Carrillo, Crockett's life is traced from his childhood to his final days at the Alamo. Of Crockett's death: "Davy and the other men fought with guns, knives, and fists until not a man among them was still alive."

Davy Crockett Decanter
McCormick Distilleries' thirteen-inch, porcelin decanter which contained a fifth of straight bourbon whiskey. The decanter, in the shape of Crockett, was issued by the Missouri-based company in 1975 as part of its "Frontiersman" series.

Davy Crockett: Defender of the Alamo
William R. Sanford and Carl R. Green's 1966 book. Of Crockett's death: "Davy Crockett died a hero's death that day in 1836."

Davy Crockett Drive-In
Trenton-by-the-Sea, Maine-based eatery in the 1950s which featured over two dozen Davy Crockett menu selections including the "Davy Crockett Mountain Top," a cocoanut ice cream sundae with chocolate sauce.

Davy Crockett Dulcimer Society
Crockett, Texas-based acoustic music organization whose members specialize in folk, western swing, gospel, Appalachian folk, and other American styles.

Davy Crockett—Explained and Defined

Harry B. Roberts' independently-produced booklets from the late 1980s (no date cited in either volumes one or two) about the Crockett of history and legend. Roberts provides no details of his death at the Alamo but states: "He had been through too many perilous experiences to recoil for the specter of death."

Davy Crockett Federal Savings Bank

Defunct Texas savings and loan which was cited by the Office of Thrift Supervision as a financial institution with "the largest number of affiliated persons ever involved with an enforcement action with a single thrift." The June 1993 issue of *United States Banker* referred to the bank as "Davy Crooked."

Davy Crockett: From the Backwoods of Tennessee to the Alamo

Stewart H. Holbrook's 1955 book about the legendary frontier hero.

Davy Crockett, Frontier Adventurer

Matthew G. Grant's 1974 children's book about the famous Tennessean. Grant traces Crockett's life "from the time he was eight" until his death at the Alamo. Of Crockett's death: "Fighting hand to hand, the Alamo defenders died to the last man."

Davy Crockett: Frontier Fighter

Lee Bishop's lusty, fictional 1983 tale about Crockett's exploits during the Creek Indian War. Crockett's passion for the ladies is so strong in this paperback that its title could have been changed to *Davy Crockett: Frontier Lover.*

Davy Crockett: Frontier Fighter

Avon Publications' comic book series of the 1950s.

Davy Crockett Frontiersman

Daily and Sunday comic strip that ran from 1955 to 1957. *Davy Crockett Frontiersman* was drawn by several different artists during its run, including Frederic Ray, who drew the art for the 1955 booklet *The Story of The Alamo.*

ISSUE #105

JUNE 1997

$5.00

THE ALAMO JOURNAL

Davy Crockett – A Snapshot of 1834.

The Official Publication of THE ALAMO SOCIETY

"Davy Crockett at the end of the Creek War" illustration by Gary Zaboly.

Davy Crockett: Frontiersman and Indian Scout

Hazel D. Davis' colorful 1955 children's book. The book, which is delightfully illustrated by William Moyers, emphasizes the famous Tennessean's life before his political career and his departure to Texas. Of Crockett's death: "Davy Crockett fell in the thickest of the fight with broken Betsy in his hand."

Davy Crockett: Gentleman From the Cane

James C. Kelly and Frederick S. Voss' 1986 glossy booklet, which accompanied the Exhibition Commemorating Crockett's Life and Legend on the 200th Anniversary of His Birth at the Tennessee State Museum.

"Davy Crockett Goes to Congress"

The second episode of the popular Walt Disney 1954-1955 television trilogy. The episode, which aired on January 26, 1955, and starred Fess Parker in the title role, traces Crockett's life from the time of his first wife's death in 1815 to the end of his congressional career in 1835.

"Davy Crockett: Guardian Spirit"

Third episode of the new "Davy Crockett" series which was broadcast on *The Magical World of Disney* in 1989. Tim Dunigan played Crockett.

Davy Crockett: Hero of the Alamo

Sanford Tousey's 1948 children's book. Of Crockett's death following his capture: "He suffered the same fate as his mates when a dozen swords entered his fighting body."

Davy Crockett: Hero of the Wild Frontier

Elizabeth R. Moseley's 1991 book for young readers, which traces Crockett's life from his childhood to his final days at the Alamo. The book is nicely illustrated by Thomas Beecham. Of Crockett's death: "Davy Crockett and Jim Bowie, with all the others, fought on bravely until the last man fell. Davy lay dead, Old Betsy by his side."

Davy Crockett Historical Society

Tennessee-based organization formed in 1889 to celebrate the 103rd anniversary of Crockett's birthday. The original Limestone, Tennessee, 1889 celebration invitation stated that "Preparations are being made to have the grandest demonstration ever held in east Tennessee." The Davy Crockett Historical Society did not continue its annual commemorations. However, in 1957, the Limestone Ruritan Club revived the celebration and has held it every year since at the Davy Crockett Birthplace State Park.

Davy Crockett Hook & Ladder Company

Poughkeepsie, New York-located fire company that was created in the late nineteenth century. In 1897 the company issued a firefighting ribbon as a special community service award.

Davy Crockett Hootenanny Song Album

Thirty-page collection of popular folk songs published by Walt Disney in 1963. The booklet, which featured a photo of Fess Parker, star of *Davy Crockett King of the Wild Frontier* on the cover, featured songs that were popular during the American folk revival of the early 1960s including "Lemon Tree," and "500 Miles," among others.

Davy Crockett: Hunter, Wit, and Patriot

Title of ninety-six-page paperback volume published by the New York-based publication firm of Beadle and Company in 1861. The cover of the publication featured Crockett at the Alamo.

"Davy Crockett, Indian Fighter"

The first episode of the popular Walt Disney 1954-1955 television trilogy. The episode, which aired December 15, 1954, focused on Crockett's participation in the Creek Indian War of 1813-1814.

Davy Crockett, Indian Fighter

Dell Comic book (#631) based on the 1954 Disneyland television episode "Davy Crockett, Indian Fighter."

Davy Crockett: Indian Fighter

Barbara Hazen's 1975 paperback which was based on Tom Blackburn's script for the first episode of Walt Disney's *Davy Crockett, King of the Wild Frontier* in 1954.

Davy Crockett Indian Scout

Cowboys and Indians movie of 1950 (Phoenix Films) starring George Montgomery in the title role as a "cousin of the Davy Crockett of Alamo fame." Interestingly, supporting actor Robert ("Lone Eagle") Barrat played Davy Crockett in the 1939 film *Man of Conquest*.

Davy Crockett in the Great Keelboat Race

Dell Comic book (#664) based upon the 1955 Disneyland television episode "Davy Crockett's Keelboat Race."

Davy Crockett, King of the Wild Frontier

Walt Disney's 1955 theatrical release of the three edited 1954-1955 television episodes: "Davy Crockett, Indian Fighter;" "Davy Crockett Goes to Congress;" "Davy Crockett at the Alamo." The ninety-three-minute film is available in the videocasette format.

Davy Crockett, King of the Wild Frontier

"Giant" sized 1955 Dell Comic book based on Walt Disney's Davy Crockett, King of the Wild Frontier.

Davy Crockett, King of the Wild Frontier

Two-part Walt Disney film strip adaptation of *Davy Crockett, King of the Wild Frontier.* This title, which is part of Disney's "Stories in American History" educational series, includes a four-page guide and an accompanying sound track on two audiocassettes and two phonograph records.

Davy Crockett King of the Wild Frontier Playset

Plastic toy set (complete name: Walt Disney's Official Davy Crockett King of the Wild Frontier Playset) first manufactured by the Marx Toy Company in 1955 during the Davy Crockett craze. Various sets, which featured Crockett at the Alamo, were issued by Marx during the 1950s, one even substituting Indians instead of Mexicans (set #3530). Additional sets were numbered #3534, #3539, #3540, #3543, #3544, and #3546. Marx reissued set #3534R in 1995 through Sears stores nationwide, and later issued a special #3534R set itself.

Davy Crockett: Le Coureur Des Bois
French publication written by Leo Lenvers in 1984.

Davy Crockett, Legendary Frontier Hero
Walter Blair's 1986 book (complete title: *Davy Crockett, Legendary Frontier Hero: His True Life Story And The Fabulous Tall Tales Told About Him*) which includes several lithograph reproduction pages from the mid-nineteenth century *Davy Crockett's Almanack* series. The book is esentially a reprint of his 1955 title. Blair devotes a number of pages to the various contemporary accounts of Crockett's death and concludes: "Arms folded, the prisoner and Davy stood straight and unflinching, staring defiantly at the Mexicans. They were shot down."

Davy Crockett Long Hunters
Tennessee-based muzzleloading organization which currently promotes living history activities at David Crockett State Park in Lawrenceburg, Tennessee.

"Davy Crockett Mambo"
Irving Fields Trio parody of "The Ballad of Davy Crockett." The musical group's 1955 Fiesta Records release was based upon the original George Bruns and Tom Blackburn composition.

Davy Crockett Masonic Lodge
San Antonio, Texas-based Freemasons lodge (#1225).

Davy Crockett Meets Death Hug
Ron Fontes and Justine Korman's 1993 children's book in the Disney "American Frontier" series, in which Crockett makes friends with a large bear called "Death Hug."

Davy Crockett Memorial Park
Thirty-five acre wooded park featuring picnic areas, playgrounds and tennis courts located in Crockett, Texas.

Davy Crockett Monument
Statue in town square of Ozona, Texas, the seat of Crockett County. The larger-than-life statue of Crockett rests on a base that is inscribed with "Be Sure You Are Right, Then Go Ahead."

Davy Crockett: Or, Be Sure You're Right, Then Go Ahead
Frank Murdock and Frank Mayo's nineteenth century play about the famous frontiersman. Mayo starred as Crockett during a run from 1872, when the play premiered, until 1896, when the actor died. A late nineteenth century testimonial penned by O. B. Frothingham of New York City noted that the play was "a very finished and beautiful piece of art."

"Davy Crockett: The Making of a Folk Hero"
Lowell H. Harrison's song which was included on *Kentucky Folklore Record* (#15) in 1969.

Davy Crockett: The Man, The Legend, The Legacy, 1786-1986
Excellent collection of essays edited by Michael A. Lofaro. The book included chapters on "The Man in the Buckskin Hunting Shirt: Fact and Fiction in the Crockett Story" by Richard Boyd Hauck, "The Recycled Hero: Walt Disney's Davy Crockett" by Margaret King, and "The Hidden 'Hero' of the Nashville Crockett Almanacs" by the editor.

Davy Crockett National Forest
Texas state park of 161,500 acres in Houston and Trinity Counties.

Davy Crockett Nuclear Bazooka
A surface-to-surface nuclear missile which contained a warhead weighing approximately 50-55 pounds. Manufactured between 1956 and 1963, the "Davy Crockett" was first deployed in 1961. It was supposedly the lightest nuclear projecticle in the American arsenal at the time. However, enlisted personnel had to dig foxholes or trenches prior to firing the "Davy Crockett"

because they could possibly be subject to the nuclear blast or radioactive fallout.

Davy Crockett on the Mississippi

William Hanna and Joseph Barbera-produced animated feature which aired on CBS-television in October 1977. The story weaves the tale of Davy Crockett, his pet bear "Honeysuckle," Mike Fink, and orphan Matt Henry, who is searching for his uncle. Andrew Jackson and a Shawneee chief named Grey Eagle also appear in this delightful story for young people. *Davy Crockett on the Mississippi* was released on videocassette in 1987.

"Davy Crockett Pure Old Bourbon"

Mid-twentieth century alcoholic beverage marketed by Hey, Grauherholz & Co. of San Francisco. The twelve-inch tall, amber bottle features the raised inscription "Davy Crockett Pure Old Bourbon."

Davy Crockett Ranch

Euro Disney's 595-room hotel at Marne-La-Vallee, France. The Davy Crockett Ranch features "Crockett's Tavern," a restaurant; "Crockett's Saloon," a snack bar; and the "Alamo Trading Post."

Davy Crockett Rifle Frolic

Ojai, California-based flintlock shoot-em-up hosted by film director-producer David Zucker, a major collector of David Crockett letters and memorabilia. Zucker has held frolics at his ranch in 1989, 1991, 1992, 1994, 1996, and 1999. Fess Parker, star of *Davy Crockett, King of the Wild Frontier,* was the featured guest at the 1991 Frolic.

Davy Crockett Roadhouse

Manchester, Tennessee-located restaurant which features printed stories about Crockett's life in each dining booth. The facility's bar is known as the "John Crockett Tavern" and the menu features such items as the "Davy Crockett 9 oz. Special Sirloin," "Davy's Classic Burger," and "Crockett Taters."

"Davy Crockett Says"

Title of 1955 Walt Disney-copyrighted newspaper column series which featured photos from *Davy Crockett, King of the Wild Frontier* and nineteenth century images. The text which accompanied each photo or image was part story-part moral, reminding kids of the 1950s, for example, that "A man has to do right by his country [and] to do right by his family."

Davy Crockett Schools

Public schools in Tennessee and Texas named after the buckskin hero. Among the dozens of educational institutions that have carried the Crockett name is the Davy Crockett elementary school in Dallas, Texas, which was featured in the April 25, 1955, *Life* magazine article "U.S. Again Is Subdued By Davy." Crockett elementary schools in Goose Creek, Houston, and San Angelo, Texas, were four star-rated schools by *Texas Monthly* in 1996.

Davy Crockett Spring

Located in Crockett, Texas, the still-flowing spring is alleged to be the 1836 campsite of the famous frontiersman as he made his way to San Antonio. A historical plaque designates the site.

Davy Crockett Stamp

A 1967 first class postage stamp issued by the United States Post Office. The five-cent stamp, which was created by New York-based artist Robert Bode and first issued in San Antonio, Texas, on August 17, 1967, Crockett's 181st birthday, features a partial-silhouette Crockett in buckskins and coonskin cap, cradling a rifle in his left hand. The United States Post Office made an initial printing of 120 million Davy Crockett stamps. In the 1990s, an enlarged version of the stamp was manufactured as a decorative magnet by Omnitech Designs in Gainesville, Florida.

Davy Crockett Stamp Books

A pair of Walt Disney-licensed stamp books distributed to retailers in 1955. The *Davy Crockett, King of the Wild Frontier*

Stamp Book featured sixty Kodachrome color stamps "from the Famous Motion Picture." However, a few of the images were promotional shots that were not included in the production. *The Davy Crockett and Mike Fink Stamp Book* featured fifty color drawing stamps created by artist Mel Crawford.

Davy Crockett Steam Fire Company No. 1
    New Orleans, Louisiana-based volunteer fire company (formed in 1841) which claims to be the nation's "oldest continuous active volunteer fire company in the U.S.A." The company has been celebrated over the years in Mardi Gras doubloons and folk art woodcrafts.

Davy Crockett Storybook
    Landoll company's 1995 children's book (no author identified) which traces Crockett on a ficticious winter hunting trip. The book stated that "Davy was considered one of the bravest men on the American frontier."

Davy Crockett Western Set
    Cowboy and Indians plastic playset made by the Plastic Art Toy Corp. of America in East Paterson, New Jersey, during the mid-1950s.

Davy Crockett Wilderness Set
    A modern-day (1990s) plastic playset made by Barzso Playsets of Illinois. The set features pioneers, Indians, a stockade fort complete with cabins, and other miscellaneous pieces.

Davy Crockett: The Untold Story
    Frank A. Driskill's 1981 children's book about Crockett's life and his friendship with the Gossett family. Of Crockett's death: "The last to go was Davy Crockett. He had no powder left and used Betsy as a club. He stood there, one arm useless. He had a deep gash in his cheek where he had been cut by a saber. At his feet were the bodies of many Mexicans who had failed in an attempt to reach him in hand-to-hand-combat. His Bowie knife, a gift from Jim Bowie, had served him well."

Davy Crockett: Sioux Slaughter
David Thompson's 1997 fictional paperback about Crockett's exploits with the Indians and the buffalo of the Great Plains.

Davy Crockett: Young Pioneer
Luarence Santrey's 1983 children's booklet which devotes every page, save the last, to Crockett's youthful exploits. The last page summarizes his adult life in one paragraph.

Davy Crockett: Young Rifleman
Aileen Wells Park's 1949 children's book which concentrates on Crockett's childhood. The book essentially skips the famous Tennessean's congressional career except for a few paragraph's in the final chapter devoted to the Alamo. Of Crockett's death: "Davy and a few others were driven back into the inner rooms of the Alamo. When their ammunition gave out, they used their guns as clubs. Not a man surrendered."

Davy Crockett Craze, The
Paul Anderson's 1996 tribute (complete title: *The Davy Crockett Craze: A Look at the 1950's Phenomenon and Davy Crockett Collectibles*) to Walt Disney's 1954-1955 television series *Davy Crockett, King of the Wild Frontier.* The text is embellished with dozens of photos (in both color and black & white) of Crockett memorabilia from the collections of two members of The Alamo Society: Dr. Murray Weissmann and Alan Kude.

Davy Crockett's Boy Hunter
Edward Willett's 1908 title in the Beadles Frontier Series. *Davy Crockett's Boy Hunter* was number eleven of 100 titles in the Cleveland, Ohio-based Arthur Westbrook Publishing Company's pulp series for young readers. The title page and all the subsequent pages identify the ten-cent publication as "David Crockett's Boy Hunter" and the cover features the young frontiersman fighting a bear with a knife and an anachronistic revolver.

Davy Crockett's Earthquake
William O. Steele's 1956 children's book.

Davy Crockett's Fiddle
Instrument owned by Crockett and inscribed "This fiddle is my property, Davy Crockett, Franklin County, Tenn. Feb. 14, 1819." The instrument was a centerpiece at the San Antonio, Texas-located Witte Museum in 1986. More importantly, it is a rare example of Crockett using the name "Davy" instead of David. It was supposedly used on Red River Dave's Decca recording "When Davy Crockett Met the San Antonio Rose" in 1955.

"Davy Crockett's Keelboat Race"
Fourth episode in the 1954-1955 television series Davy Crockett, King of the Wild Frontier. In the episode, Crockett races against Mike Fink to see who can reach New Orleans first.

Davy Crockett's Vow, or, His Last Shot for Vengeance
Kit Clyde's 1886 "dime novel."

Day After Roswell, The
Col. Philip J. Corso (ret.) and William J. Birnes' 1996 book about an alleged federal government UFO coverup that features the words of Davy Crockett. The book begins and ends with Crockett's famous motto: "Be sure you're right, then go ahead."

Dead Game, or, Davy Crockett's Double
"Old Scout" 1906 "dime novel" in the Pluck and Luck series.

Death of a Legend
Bill Groneman's 1999 book (complete title: *Death of a Legend: The Myth and Mystery Surrounding the Death of Davy Crockett*) about the historic debate concerning Davy Crockett's death at the Alamo. The author traces the controversy from 1836 when the first conflicting accounts of the famous frontiersman's death appeared in American newspapers. The book also summarizes the debate over Crockett's death during the 1990s

which has been examined in such publications as *Wild West, The Alamo Journal,* and *Military History of the West.*

Death of a Legend
Artist Don Griffiths' 1993 canvas depicting the final moments of Crockett at the Alamo. The painting first appeared on the cover of Bill Groneman's 1994 book *Defense of a Legend.*

Death of Crockett
John Hull's 1994 acrylic on canvas which was first displayed at the Grace Borgenicht Gallery in New York City on September 8, 1994.

Death of Davy Crockett
Brian Huberman-created 1993 video documentary, which includes a broad overview of the Alamo in art and film. Huberman and co-producer Edward Hugetz utilize a rich combination of original images, character voice-overs, interviews, and period music to tell of the famous frontiersman's final days and subsequent legend.

Defense of a Legend
Bill Groneman's 1994 book (complete title: *Defense of a Legend: Crockett and the de la Peña Diary*) about the arguments concerning Crockett's death at the Alamo. The author criticizes the authenticity of the José Enrique de la Peña account, which suggests that Crockett was captured at the Battle of the Alamo and subsequently executed.

Derose, Anthony Lewis
Nineteenth-century artist who created an 1834 watercolor on paper of David Crockett. Artist Asher B. Durand made an engraving in 1834 based on DeRose's original.

Derr, Mark
Author of the 1993 book, *The Frontiersman: The Real Life and Many Legends of Davy Crockett.*

Dickinson, George W.

Mid-nineteenth century book dealer who wrote a letter in Gallatin, Tennessee, to a friend on April 11, 1836, suggesting a different death for Davy Crockett: "We understand that the great man Crockett is dead. He went to Texas to fight the Spanairds and Indians which took the Fort and we understand that Crockett killed himself."

Direct Descendants of David Crockett

International organization of the Crockett family which was founded in Tennessee in 1981. The first organizational meeting of the group was held in Greeneville, Tennessee, in 1984. The Direct Descendants of David Crockett hold reunions every other year, alternating between Tennessee and Texas. The organization publishes a periodic newsletter called *Go Ahead.*

Disneyland

Anaheim, California-based theme park which opened in 1955 with Fess Parker, star of "Davy Crockett," leading the opening-day parade. Crockett was celebrated in numerous ways over the years at Disneyland, especially in the 1950s when the Davy Crockett Museum was the centerpiece for visiting Crockett fans in Frontierland. The museum was replaced by other frontier-related enterprises over the decades.

DisneyWorld

Orlando, Florida-based theme park which primarily acknowledges Davy Crockett at the Crockett Tavern located in the Fort Wilderness Campground. The tavern features an oil painting of Fess Parker as Crockett by Jim Noble, printed lyrics to "Farewell," and a printed congressional speech among several other items. In 1989, following the broadcast of the new Disney Davy Crockett television series a year earlier, a costumed DisneyWorld cast member was featured as Crockett during the afternoon parade at the Magic Kingdom. In the early 1990s, the theme park closed the Davy Crockett Canoes attraction at Frontierland. However, the Magic Kingdom still sells coonskin caps and Davy Crockett toy rifles. Crockett's Tavern, a restaurant-bar, is located at the Fort Wilderness Resort.

Dooley, Elliot
Author of the 1991 hard-bound comic book, *Davy Crockett.*

Dorson, Richard M.
Editor of the 1939 book *Davy Crockett: American Comic Legend.*

Driskill, Frank A.
Author of the 1981 children's book, *Davy Crockett: The Untold Story.*

Dunn, Harvey
Esquire magazine artist in the 1950s who painted *There Was a Man: Davy Crockett Fought His Way to Glory on the Wall of the Alamo.*

Dutchess of York
Member of the British family who wore a coonskin cap during part of a twelve-day sojourn of Canada in 1987. One British publication gave her a new title: "Fergie Crockett, Queen of the Wild Frontier."

Eggleston, George Cary
Author of the 1875 book *David Crockett.*

Ellis, Edward S.
Author (occasionally used pen name of Charles E. Lasalle) of several nineteenth century Crockett titles for young readers including *The Texas Trailer; or, Davy Crockett's Last Bear Hunt* (1871), *The Bear-Hunter; or, Davy Crockett as a Spy* (1873), *The Life of Colonel David Crockett* (1876),and *Col. Crockett, the Bear King* (1886).

Evatt, Harriet
Author of the 1955 children's book *Davy Crockett, Big Indian, and Little Bear.*

F

Fabulous David Crockett, The

Ernest T. Thompson's 1956 booklet (complete title: *The Fabulous David Crockett; His Life and Times in Gibson County, Tenn. Including Tall Tales and Anecdotes of the Western Wilds*) about the famous Tennessean. Of Crockett's death: ". . . Crockett was killed at the Alamo, where he fought until the very last."

Fall of the Alamo, The

Robert James Onderdonk's 1903 painting which features Davy Crockett as its central figure. The five-by-seven-foot canvas, which was displayed at the St. Louis World's Fair in 1904, currently hangs in the Texas Governor's Mansion in Austin, Texas.

Farewell

Song written by David Crockett and set to music by George Bruns, co-author of "The Ballad of Davy Crockett," in 1954. Fess Parker sang the composition in "Davy Crockett at the Alamo," which was initially broadcast on American television on February 23, 1955.

Farnum, Dustin

Actor who played the title role in the 1916 motion picture *Davy Crockett*. Farnum's brother, William, played Sam Houston in the 1917 film, *The Conqueror.*

Farr, Naunerle C.

Author of the 1979 children's dual biography, *Davy Crockett/ Daniel Boone.*

Feely, Thomas F., Jr.

Creator of the high-detailed diorama "Crockett's Last Stand" and co-author (with Nancy E. Nagle) of the 1995 booklet, *Crockett's Last Stand—A Diorama.* Feely has also created a number of individual Crockett figures over the years for military and western history collectors.

Fess Parker Winery and Vineyard

Los Olivos, California-based winery established by Fess Parker, star of Walt Disney's *Davy Crockett, King of the Wild Frontier.* Parker purchased 714 acres in the San Ynez Valley in 1987 and bottled his first vintage two years later. Parker's respected and award-winning wines are graced by labels which feature a small coonskin cap. In addition to his wines, the Fess Parker Winery and Vineyard also offers such tasty gifts as "Crockett's Roasted Garlic Salsa," "Davy's Wrangler Seasonin,'" and "Wild Frontiers Chipotle Grill Sauce."

Fifty-seventh Militia Regiment

Tennesse military unit of Lawrence County in which Crockett commanded as a colonel in 1818.

Finley, Mary ("Polly")

Crockett's first wife, daughter of William and Jean Finley. She was probably born in 1788. Crockett married Finley on August 14, 1806, two days before his twentieth birthday. Polly Crockett gave birth to three children: John Wesley (1807), William (1809), and Margaret (1815). She died in 1815.

Fitzgerald, William

Pro-Andrew Jackson candidate who defeated Crockett in the 1831 congressional election. Crockett referred to Fitzgerald as "the thing that had the name of beating me."

Fontes, Ron

Co-author (with Justine Korman) of the 1992 children's book *Davy Crockett and the Highwaymen,* and 1993 children's book, *Davy Crockett Meets Death Hug.*

Ford, Anne

Author of the 1961 children's book *Davy Crockett: A See and Read Biography.*

Ford, "Tennessee" Ernie

Singer who scored a top five hit on the *Billboard* record charts with "The Ballad of Davy Crockett" in 1955.

Ford, Francis

Actor who is traditionaly known to have portrayed Davy Crockett in the 1911 silent film *The Immortal Alamo*. Ford is the older brother of famous film director John Ford. According to film historian Frank Thompson, Francis Ford may not have actually played Crockett in the film, which also had been distributed under the title *Fall of the Alamo*. As a matter of fact, there may not even have been an actual Crockett character in the film.

Foreman, Gary L.

Author of the 1986 glossy booklet, *Crockett: The Gentleman From the Cane,* and producer of the "Davy Crockett Birthday Party" living history program held on the grounds of the Witte Museum in San Antonio, Texas, on August 17, 1986. Foreman was also a featured historian in the Arts & Entertainment network's 1994 "Biography" episode, *Davy Crockett: American Frontier Legend.*

Forgotten Pioneer, The; The Life of Davy Crockett

Marion Michael Null's 1954 book. Of Crockett's death: "One by one, asking no quarter, fighting to the end until not a man was left. Thus died Colonel Davy Crockett and one hundred and eighty-two men."

Fort Crockett

Galveston, Texas-located American artillery installation. Fort Crockett was built in 1897 and closed in 1947.

"Four Loves Had Davy Crockett"

Irving Stone's multi-part romantic story which appeared in the *American Weekly* during the late spring of 1955. Crockett's four loves included "The Kennedy Girl," "Polly," "Margaret," and "Elizabeth."

Frank, Janet

Author of the 1955 children's book *Davy Crockett and the Indians.*

Frontiersman, The: The Real Life and Many Legends of Davy Crockett

Mark Derr's 1993 biography. The author makes several erroneous assumptions in his first chapter about the popular Walt Disney 1954-1955 television Crockett series. For example, Derr states that the first episode's Indians were actually "white men in greasepaint." However, with the exception of Chief Red Stick (Pat Hogan), all the Indians in the "Creek Indian War" episode were Native Americans! Derr suggests that Crockett was killed following his capture by Mexican troops at the Alamo on March 6, 1836.

Frontier Woman, The Daughter of Davy Crockett
Title of 1956 motion picture starring Cindy Carson, Lance Fuller, and Ann Kelly.

Garland, Hamlin
Author who penned the intro to the 1923 "Modern Student's Library" title, *The Autobiography of David Crockett*.

G.I. Joe
Famous toy soldier issued as a limited Davy Crockett souvenir "Alamo Patrol" figure at the 1998 G.I. Joe Convention held in San Antonio, Texas. The Crockett figure was outfitted with a buckskin coat, trousers, shirt, tie, boots, coonskin cap, buckskin shoulder pouch, rifle, and powder horn. Only 100 of the "Alamo Patrol" sets were made. Each set also included a Mexican *soldado*.

Gibson, John H.
Military commander of a scouting expedition against the Creeks in which Crockett participated during the early autumn of 1813. Gibson served as a major under Col. John Coffee's command.

"Go Ahead"
The simplified version of Crockett's famous motto: "Be sure you're right, then go ahead."

"Go Ahead"—A March Dedicated to Colonel Crockett
Sheet music published in 1835 by the New York-based firm of Firth and Hall.

Go Ahead Davie

Hugh Poindexter's 1936 book about Crockett in his pre-Alamo days. The British-produced publication uses the name "Davie" instead of Davy.

Grant, Bruce

Author of the 1955 children's book, *Davy Crockett: American Hero.*

Grant, Matthew G.

Author of the 1974 children's book *Davy Crockett, Frontier Adventurer.*

Green, Carl R.

Co-author (with William R. Sanford) of the 1966 book *Davy Crockett; Defender of the Alamo.*

Greenman, George

Shipbuilder whose firm built the clipper ship *Davy Crockett* in 1853.

Greenway, Shirley

Co-author (with Felicity Trotman) of the 1986 children's book, *Davy Crockett.*

Griffith, James

Veteran character actor who played Davy Crockett in *The First Texan,* a 1956 film starring Joel McCrea as Sam Houston.

Griffiths, Don

Artist who painted the 1993 canvas *Death of A Legend,* which depicts the final moments of Crockett at the Alamo.

Groneman, Bill

Author of *Defense of a Legend: Crockett and the de la Peña Diary,* and *Death of a Legend.* Groneman also also authored a number of articles about Crockett in various publications, including *The Alamo Journal, Roundup* magazine, and *Military History of the West,* among others.

Gwynne, Fred
Actor who played Davy Crockett in the 1971 *You Are There* television episode "The Siege of the Alamo" in 1971.

Hackett, James
Actor who played the Davy Crockett-like character Nimrod Wildfire in James Kirke Paulding's 1831 play *The Lion of the West*. Crockett actually viewed Hackett in the play during an 1833 performance in Washington, D.C.

Hamsely, Col. Bob
Co-author (with Judge John Morrison) of the 1955 booklet *The Real . . . David Crockett, Authentic and Illustrated.*

Harding, Ben
Alter-ego of Kentucky Congressman Ben Hardin who evolved into a rival of the almanac Davy Crockett in the 1830s. Harding's character even appeared in the almanacs with Crockett. Both graced the cover of the 1845 *Davy Crockett's Almanac*.

Harper, Herbert
Editor of *Houston and Crockett; Heroes of Tennessee and Texas, an Anthology.*

Harris, Flavius
Fictional sidekick of Davy Crockett in David Thompson's paperback series on the famous frontier hero. Harris teams up with Davy in *Homecoming* (1997), *Sioux Slaughter* (1997), *Blood Hunt* (1997), *Mississippi Mayhem* (1997), *Blood Rage* (1997), *Comanche Country* (1998), *Texican Terror* (1998), and *Cannibal Country* (1998).

Harrison, Lowell
Author of "Davy Crockett: The Making of a Folk Hero," a song which was featured on the 1969 recording *Kentucky Folklore Record* (#15).

Hauck, Richard Boyd
Author of the informative 1982 *Crockett: A Bio-Bibliography.*

Hazen, Barbara
Author of the 1975 paperback, *Davy Crockett: Indian Fighter.*

Hogue, Albert Ross
Author of *Davy Crockett and Others in Fentress County Who Have Given the Country a Prominent Place in History.*

Holbrook, Stewart H.
Author of the 1955 book *Davy Crockett: From the Backwoods of Tennessee to the Alamo.*

Homecoming
First book in David Thompson's historical fiction series on Davy Crockett. In *Homecoming* (1997), Crockett travels to the Great Lakes, saves a Chippewa squaw, and battles the Indians of the Midwest.

How Davy Crockett Got a Bearskin Coat
Wyatt Blassingame's 1972 children's publication.

How Did Davy Die?
Dan Kilgores's controversial 1978 publication about the death of Crockett. Kilgore's book, which relied primarily on Mexican accounts of the Battle of the Alamo, originated as an address delivered to the Texas State Historical Association on March 4, 1977. Kilgore, who served as president of the association, revised and expanded his address into the forty-eight-page *How Did Davy Die?* Kilgore concluded that the reports of seven Mexican accounts, especially the writings of José Enrique de la Peña, indicated that Crockett was one of a small number of Alamo defenders who were captured and subsequently executed.

Huberman, Brian
Rice University-based associate professor of Art and Art History who has chonicled the story of Davy Crockett and the Alamo on video since 1974. His forty-minute documentary on the making of John Wayne's *The Alamo* was included in the 1992

"director's cut" video release of the 1960 epic motion picture. In 1993, he produced (along with Edward Hugetz) *The Death of Davy Crockett,* a lengthy video overview of the famous frontiersman and the Alamo. Huberman recently completed a new video study of Crockett.

Huddle, William Henry
Nineteenth century painter of *David Crockett,* a work which depicts a standing buckskined Crockett. Currently held by the Archives Division of the Texas State Library.

Hull, John
Artist who painted the 1994 acrylic on canvas *Death of Crockett.*

Hunnicutt, Arthur
Actor who played Davy Crockett in the 1955 motion picture *The Last Command.*

Hutton, Paul Andrew
University of New Mexico history professor who wrote the introduction to the 1987 edition of *A Narrative of the Life of David Crockett of the State of Tennessee.* Hutton, who has written a number of articles about Crockett in various publications, also wrote "Sunrise in His Pocket," an essay about the Crockett almanacs in the 1997 book *Frontier and Region,* which he co-edited (with Robert C. Ritchie). In addition, he was one of the featured historians in the Arts & Entertainment network's 1994 "Biography" episode, *Davy Crockett: American Frontier Legend.* Hutton is preparing a major biography on Crockett.

Hyman, Rob
Keyboardist-vocalist with The Hooters ("And We Danced") who stated that he "got hooked on music after learning to play the Davy Crockett theme on the piano at age three."

In Texas with Davy Crockett
John T. McIntyre's 1926 children's book.

In Texas With Davy Crockett: A Story of the Texas War of Independence
Everett McNeil's 1908 children's book.

Indian Removal Bill
Andrew Jackson administration legislation which forced Native American tribes of the Southeast to relocate west of the Mississippi River. Despite his participation in the Creek Indian War, Crockett denounced the bill and Jackson's support of it.

Jackson, Andrew
President of the United States as a result of his victories in the elections of 1828 and 1832. Crockett served under Jackson in the Creek Indian War and originally supported him as president. However, he later split with "Old Hickory" over such issues as Indian removal, squatters' rights, the "Spoils System," and the National Bank. Crockett referred to Jackson as "My Dog."

Jackson Gazette
Madison County, Tennessee-based newspaper which played a pivotal role in Crockett's congressional defeat in 1831.

Jacobs, John L.
Finley Gap, Tennessee, neighbor of the Crocketts who in 1884 described the famous frontiersman in the following manner: "He was about six feet high, weighed about two hundred pounds, had no surplus flesh, broad shouldered, stood erect, was a man of great physical strength, of fine appearnace, his cheeks mantled with a rosy hue, eyes vivaciousness, and in form, had no superior."

Jeffries, Jeff
Author of *Remember the Alamo! The Story of Davy Crockett.*

Jersey City, New Jersey
Site of May 2, 1834, rifle frolic in which Crockett participated. This may have been the most northern location where Crockett fired a rifle.

Jones, Francis
Commander of the Tennessee Volunteer Mounted Riflemen, a unit Crockett joined during the Creek Indian War. Captain Jones was the unit's leader when Crockett enlisted as a private for a ninety-day term of service commencing on September 24, 1813.

Judd, Cameron
Author of the 1994 paperback, *Crockett of Tennessee.*

Kanawah, David
Alamo movie set reconstruction team member who doubled for actor Merrill (David Crockett) Connally during the final battle sequence of the 1988 IMAX motion picture *Alamo . . . The Price of Freedom.*

Keith, Brian
Actor who played Davy Crockett in the 1987 television movie *The Alamo: 13 Days to Glory.*

Kellogg, Steven
Author and illustrator of the 1995 children's book *Sally Ann Thunder Ann Whirlwind Crockett.*

Kelly, James C.
Co-author (with Frederick S. Voss) of the 1986 Tennessee State Museum booklet *Davy Crockett, Gentleman From The Cane.*

"Kentuck"
Name Crockett gave his 1813 Franklin County, Tennessee, homestead.

Kentucky Headhunters
Kentucky-based country-rock quintet which released a rollicking version of "The Ballad of Davy Crockett" in 1991. Noted drummer Fred Young in an April 1991 interview in *The Alamo Journal:* "We needed to come out with 'Davy Crockett,' make it

fast, make it rock." The song, off the group's *Electric Barnyard* album, peaked at number 47 on the country charts.

Kilgore, Dan
Former president of the Texas State Historical Association in 1977, and author of the controversial 1978 publication *How Did Davy Die?* Kilgore suggested that Crockett was captured and later executed at the Alamo.

Kings and Queens Carnival Club
Organization established in 1964 which distributed silver aluminum "David Crockett, King of the Wild Frontier" doubloons at the 1980 Mardi Gras in New Orleans.

Kitchen, Benjamin
Educator who operated a school attended by the young David Crockett. The structure was located to the east of Barton's Spring, near present-day Russellville, Tennessee. Following a fight with a school mate, Crockett feared returning to the educator. In his autobiography, Crockett noted: ". . . if I was turned over to this old Kitchen, I should be cooked up to a cracklin, in little or not time."

Kittredge, Belden
Author of the 1945 children's book *The Truth about Casey Jones And other Fabulous America heroes, including Johnny Appleseed, Davy Crockett, Roy Bean, and Mike Fink.*

Korman, Justine
Author of the 1991 children's books, *Davy Crockett and the Creek Indians, Davy Crockett at the Alamo,* and co-author (with Ron Fontes) of *Davy Crockett Meets Death Hug.*

Landis, Cullen
Actor who played the title role in the 1926 motion picture *Davy Crockett at the Fall of The Alamo.*

Lasalle, Charles E.
Pen name of Edward S. Ellis who wrote *The Texas Trailer, or*

Davy Crockett's Last Bear Hunt, an 1871 Beadles and Adams "dime novel." The publication was reprinted in 1878 as *Col. Crockett, the Texan Trailer.* As Lasalle, Ellis also authored *The Bear Hunter; or DavyCrockett as a Spy* in 1873.

Lawrence, James Duncan
Author of the 1955 children's book *Davy Crockett and the Indian Secret.*

Le Sueur, Meridel
Author of the 1951 book *Chanticleer of the Wilderness Road: A Story of Davy Crockett.*

Legends of Davy Crockett
Ardis Edwards Burton's 1955 authorized Walt Disney book for young readers. Burton's text is an adaptation of Tom Blackburn's script for the 1954-1955 television episodes *Davy Crockett, King of the Wild Frontier.* Like the original Disney production, Crockett's death at the Alamo is not detailed.

Legends of Davy Crockett, The
Sunday newspaper comic strip drawn by Jesse Marsh that ran from July 17, 1955, to January 8, 1956. Although not a Disney-strip, Marsh's Crockett was based on Fess Parker's Crockett characterization.

Lenvers, Leo
Author of the 1984 French book *Davy Crockett: Le Coureur des Bois.*

Life and Adventures of Colonel David Crockett
Title of 1864 Beadle's Dime Biographical Library booklet, essentially a reprint of the New York and London, England-based publishing firm's *Col. David Crockett, The Celebrated Hunter, Wit and Patriot,* which was printed in 1861. Unlike the 1861 title, which had no cover art, the 1864 version featured an Alamo battle scene. In the text, Crockett is identified as one of six Alamo defenders who survive the battle only to be subsequently executed. Of Crockett's death: "He died without a groan, 'a frown on his brow and a smile of scorn and defiance on his lips.'"

Life and Adventures of Colonel David Crockett of West Tennessee

Matthew St. Clair Clarke's 1833 biography of the famous frontiersman. Clarke, who had served as the clerk of the U.S. House of Representatives, embellished the popular book (also titled *Sketches and Eccentricities of Colonel David Crockett of West Tennessee*) with passages from James Kirke Paulding's *The Lion of the West,* including: "I'm . . . David Crockett, fresh from the backwoods, half-horse, half-alligator, a little touched with snapping turtle."

Life and Essays of Benjamin Franklin

Franklin's autobiography (complete title: *The Life and Essays of Benjamin Franklin written by himself*) which Crockett claimed as a model for his own 1834 autobiography. Before he departed to Texas, Crockett gave a copy of Franklin's book to W. H. Fullerton. Inside the book, Crockett wrote: "I'll leave this truth for others when I am dead. Just be sure you are right and then go ahead."

Life of David Crockett in Lawrence County

John F. Morrison's 1967 publication for the Tennessee Department of Conservation, Division of State Parks.

Life of David Crockett: The Original Humorist and Irrepressible Backwoodsman

Post-1836 book which combines Crockett's 1834 autobiography with the ghost-written (Richard Penn Smith) 1836 volume *Col. Crockett's Exploits and Adventures in Texas.* This combination book (complete title: *Life of David Crockett; The Original Humorist and Irrepressible Backwoodsman comprising His Early History; His Bear Hunting And Other Adventures; His Services In The Creek War; His Electioneering Speeches And Career In Congress; With His Triumphal Tour Through The Northern States, And Services In The Texan War to which is added An Account Of His Glorious Death At The Alamo While Fighting In Defence Of Texan Independence*) was printed by several publishers in the late nineteenth and early twentieth centuries. On the cover of one undated version published by the W. B. Conkey Company in Chicago, a dapper-looking gentleman and a lady appear to be promenading in Napoleonic French style.

The Life of Davy Crockett in Picture and Story

C. R. Schaare's 1935 children's book which features periodic illustrated panels. Of Crockett's death following his capture: "But before he could cover half the distance, a dozen swords plunged into his body."

Life of Martin Van Buren

Ghost-written Crockett book of 1835 by Augustin Smith Clayton (complete title: *The Life of Martin Vanburen, Hair-Apparent to the "Government," and the Appointed Successor of General Jackson*), which criticized Democrat Martin Van Buren, the New Yorker who served as Andrew Jackson's second vice-president. Van Buren won the presidential election of 1836.

"Li'l Davy"

Cartoon character that looked like a younger and cuter Davy Crockett which appeared in several Disney comics during 1956-1958, including *Frontierland* #1, *Donald Duck Beach Party* #3, and *Disneyland Birthday Party* #1.

Lion of the West, The

James Kirke Paulding's 1831 play which featured a frontier character called Nimrod Wildfire, who was closely associated with Crockett. David Crockett saw the play in 1833 in Washington, D.C.

Littlejohn, Elbridge Gerry

Author of the 1897 children's book *Texas History Stories; Houston, Austin, Crockett, La Salle*.

Lofaro, Michael A.

Editor of *Davy Crockett: The Man, The Legend, The Legacy, 1786-1986,* and co-editor (with Joe Cummings) of the 1989 essay collection *Crockett at Two Hundred: New Perspectives on the Man and the Myth*. Lofaro, who has also written a number of articles about Crockett in various publications, was one of the featured historians in the Arts & Entertainment network's 1994 "Biography" episode, *Davy Crockett: American Frontier Legend*.

McIntyre, John T.
Author of the 1926 children's book *In Texas With Davy Crockett.*

McKernan, Frank
Author of the 1911 book *David Crockett–Scout.*

McNeil, Everett
Author of the 1908 children's book *In Texas With Davy Crockett: A Story of the Texas War of Independence.*

Madison County
Pro-Jackson county in west Tennessee whose voters cast crucial votes against Crockett in the 1831 congressional election. Crockett managed only 429 votes against victor William Fitzgerald's 1,214. Crockett, however, defeated Fitzgerald in 1833.

Mayer, Edwin Justus
Author of the 1941 three-act play, *Sunrise in my Pocket or The Last Days of Davy Crockett: An American Saga.*

Mayo, Frank
Nineteenth-century actor who portrayed the title role of *Davy Crockett; or, Be Sure You're Right, Then Go Ahead* from 1872 to 1896. Mayo, who co-wrote the play with Frank Murdock, died in 1896.

Meadowcraft, Enid Lamonte
Author of the 1952 children's book, *The Story of Davy Crockett.*

Meine, Franklin J.
Editor of the 1955 collection *The Crockett Almanacks: Nashville Series, 1835-1838.*

Mississippi Mayhem
One of David Thompson's paperback titles in his "Davy

Crockett" series. In *Mississippi Mayhem* (1997) Crockett battles with the deadly Thunderbird, a flying creature that dominated the skies over the Mississippi River Valley.

Montgomery, George
Actor who played Crockett (actually Davy Crockett's cousin) in the 1950 motion picture *Davy Crockett Indian Scout.*

Morrison, Judge John
Co-author (with Col. Bob Hamsley) of the 1955 booklet *The Real . . . David Crockett, Authentic and Illustrated.*

Morrison, John F.
Author of the 1967 publication *Life of David Crockett in Lawrence County.*

Morrow, Temple Houston
Keynote address speaker at the unveiling of the monument to David Crockett at his old home near Trenton, Tennessee, on October 13, 1950. Morrow stated: "That one day his voice would be heard in the halls of Congress, and later he would be numbered among the immortals of the ages."

Moseley, Elizabeth
Author of the 1991 children's book *Davy Crockett: Hero of the Wild Frontier.*

Munroe, Kirk
Author of 1905 children's book *With Crockett and Bowie, or Fighting for the Lone-Star Flag.*

Murdock, Frank
Co-author (with Frank Mayo) of the long-running nineteenth century play *Davy Crockett; or, Be Sure You're Right, Then Go Ahead.*

"My Dog"
Crockett's derogatory nickname given to Andrew Jackson after the two had political disagreements.

Nacogdoches
Texas settlement where Crockett swore an oath of allegiance in 1836 "to the provisional Government of Texas, or any future republican Government that may be hereafter declared."

"Natural Man, A"
Title of the second episode of the new "Davy Crockett" series, which was broadcast on *The Magical World of Disney* in 1988. Tim Dunigan played Crockett.

Nava, John
California-based artist who created *David Crockett 1812,* the painting of a young David Crockett, in 1993.

Neagle, John
Nineteenth-century artist who is attributed as the creator of the c. 1834 oil on canvas of David Crockett.

Newsam, Albert
Nineteenth-century artist who is attributed with creating (after Samuel S. Osgood) the 1834 lithograph of David Crockett.

Null, Marion Michael
Author of the 1954 book *The Forgotten Pioneer, The Life of Davy Crockett.*

Old Whirlwind: A Story of Davy Crockett
Elizabeth Jane Coatsworth's 1953 children's book.

Onderdonk, Robert Jenkins
Painter (1852-1917) of the 1903 canvas *The Fall of the Alamo,* which features a rifle-wielding Davy Crockett. This canvas of Crockett has been the most reproduced action image of Crockett in the twentieth century.

CROCKETT

BE SURE YOU ARE RIGHT THEN GO AHEAD

David Crockett statue.
— Courtesy the Daughters of the Republic of Texas Library at the Alamo

On the Crockett Trail

Rod Timanus' 1999 book which retraces the final journey of David Crockett from his last home in Rutherford, Tennessee, to the Alamo.

Our American Pioneers: Daniel Boone, George Rogers Clark, David Crockett, Kit Carson

Francis M. Perry's 1900 children's book.

Ozona

Texas town (1990 population: 3,110) which serves as the seat of Crockett County. In fact, Ozona is the only town in Crockett County. The community features the Crockett County Memorial Park, the Crockett County Museum, and the Davy Crockett Monument.

Parker, Fess

Texas-born actor who played the title role in the Walt Disney 1954-1955 television trilogy *Davy Crockett, King of the Wild Frontier.* The three episodes were later edited together and released as a feature film in 1955. Parker also starred as Crockett in two 1955 television prequels: "Davy Crockett's Keelboat Race" and "Davy Crockett and the River Pirates." Parker's characterization of the frontier hero was voted "Best Davy Crockett" by The Alamo Society in 1989. Parker was the guest of honor at the 1994 Alamo Society Symposium in San Antonio, Texas.

Parks, Aileen Wells

Author of the 1949 children's book, *Davy Crockett: Young Rifleman.*

Parrington, Vernon Louis

American historian who wrote the respected *Main Currents of American Thought* in 1930. Parrington called Crockett "first among the Smart Alecks of the canebrakes." The historian concluded that "Davy was a good deal of wag, and the best joke he ever played upon posterity [was] that he has swallowed up the

Fess Parker as Davy Crockett © The Walt Disney Company.
— Courtesy the author's collection

myth whole and persists in setting a romantic halo on his coon-skin cap."

Patton, Elizabeth

Crockett's second wife, the widow of a Creek Indian War veteran. The two were married on May 22, 1816. Elizabeth had two children from her first marriage and gave birth to three children with David: Robert Patton (1816), Rebecca (1818), and Matilda (1821). Elizabeth died in 1860.

Paulding, James Kirke

Author of the 1831 play *The Lion of the West* which featured a frontier character called Nimrod Wildfire who was closely associated with Davy Crockett.

Pearle, Rembrandt

Artist who painted Crockett during the Tennessean's first term in Congress.

Perry, Francis M.

Author of the 1900 children's book *Our American Pioneers: Daniel Boone, George Rogers Clark, David Crockett, Kit Carson* and the 1900 Baldwin's Biographical Booklet, *The Story of David Crockett.*

Petersen, Gert

Danish researcher who has assembled an unpublished day-to-day account of Crockett in the Creek Indian War. Some of his findings have been published in *Go Ahead,* the newsletter of the Direct Descendants of David Crockett.

Picture Book of Davy Crockett, A

David A. Adler's 1996 children's book. The author identifies the conflicting accounts of Crockett's death at the Alamo but states: "Soon after he was taken prisoner, David Crockett was attacked by one dozen enemy soldiers who stabbed and killed him with their swords."

Picture Story of Davy Crockett, The

Felix Sutton's 1955 children's pamphlet. Illustrated by H. B.

Vestal, this lively treatment of Crockett's life emphasizes the famous Tennessean's youth, skips his political career, and highlights his final days at the Alamo. Of Crockett's death: "There [the Mexicans] were met by the desperate last-ditch stand of Davy Crockett and his brave companions. When the fight was over, not one American was left alive."

Poindexter, Hugh
Author of the 1936 British book *Go Ahead Davie*.

Polk, James Knox
Tennessee politician who served in the United States House of Representatives from 1825 to 1839, including Crockett's three terms during the 20th, 21st and 23rd Congresses. Polk, like Crockett, began his congressional career as loyal Jacksonian. However, Polk remained loyal to President Andrew Jackson's Democratic Party while Crockett became disillusioned with a number of administration policies. Polk became Speaker of the House of Representatives in 1835, the year Crockett lost his last congressional campaign. In 1844, Polk defeated Henry Clay for the presidency. While president, Texas became the twenty-eighth state on December 29, 1845.

Pluck and Luck
"Dime novel" series which featured a number of Crockett titles including *Davy Crockett, Jr., or, "Be Sure You're Right, Then Go Ahead,"* (1905); *Dead Game, or, Davy Crockett's Double* (1906), and *Young Davy Crockett, or, The Hero of Silver Gulch* (1917).

Pompey Smash
Popular antebellum minstrel show character who "battled" the famous Tennessee frontier hero in the song "Pompey Smash and Davy Crockett." In the song, both characters agree to stop fighting after each had swallowed the other's head.

Potter, Reuben M.
Author of *The Fall of the Alamo* in 1860 in which Crockett's death is described as being "shot down" during the battle. Twenty years later, Potter responded to an article about Crockett's sur-

render in the Woodbridge, New Jersey, newspaper *The Independent Hour* by stating: "David Crockett never surrendered to bear, tiger, Indian, or Mexican."

"Pretty Betsey"

Muzzleloading rifle presented to Crockett by the Young Whigs of Philadelphia on July 1, 1834. The fifty-caliber weapon was made by Philadelphia gunsmith Richard Constable and was fired by Crockett for the first time in Camden, New Jersey, shortly after the presentation. In the February 1988 issue of *The Alamo Journal,* Mrs. Mary Elizabeth Crockett Holderness was quoted describing the rifle: "It is a percussion cap rifle with an octagonal barrel and a stock of curly maple. Along the top of the barrel in inlaid letters of gold are the words 'Presented By The Young Men of Philadelphia to the Hon. David Crockett.' The fittings are of silver. The plate which holds the firing piece has the maker's name, Constable-Phila. The trigger guard has an alligator engraved on it. Under the wider part of the stock are three silver stars. There is also a silver band around the end of the stock which is engraved and which holds the button, which when pushed still opens the hinged silver door of the patch box. This box has engraved on it a racoon at a reed-surrounded pond. On the other side of the stock is a silver deer's head. Just in front of the trigger guard is a much worn figure in silver holding a sword drawn in one hand and, presumably, a volume in the other. At any rate, under the figure are the words 'Constitution and Law.' The barrel is approximately 40 inches in length. The rifle is approximately 56 inches."

Quit Pulling My Leg: A Story of Davy Crockett

Robert Quackenbush's 1987 children's book. Of Crockett's death: "Davy Crockett was one of the few survivors taken prisoner, as he was put to a tortuous death by sword."

"Rainbow in the Thunder"

Title of the debut episode of the new "Davy Crockett" series which was broadcast on *The Magical World of Disney* in 1988. Tim Dunigan played Crockett.

Reiter, Harriet G.

Author of the 1905 "Instructor Literature Series" booklet, *David Crockett.*

Remember the Alamo! The Story of Davy Crockett

Title of Jeff Jeffries' undated British book about Crockett's life. Despite the title, nearly half of the book's pages are devoted to Crockett's life prior to the Texas Revolution. Of Crockett's death: "A bullet struck his head, burning its way across his brow. He faltered momentarily then fell to his knees, and knew no more."

Rendezvous at the Alamo: Highlights in the Lives of Bowie, Crockett & Travis

Virgil E. Baugh's 1960 book about the Alamo's three most famous defenders. Baugh reviews several conflicting accounts of Crockett's death in his "The Myth-Makers and Military 'Experts'" section. The author suggests that Crockett could not have been captured and executed because "he would never have done" such a thing.

Retan, Walter

Author of the 1993 children's book, *The Story of Davy Crockett, Frontier Hero.*

Roberts, Harry B.

Author of the independently-produced, two-volume book-let series *Davy Crockett—Explained and Defended* published in the late 1980s (no date given in either title).

Rolling Stones

Veteran British rock and roll band sang about the famous

frontiersman on "Mean Disposition," a track off its 1995 *Voodoo Lounge* album. One lyrical line stated: "I'm gonna go out and stand my ground/Like Crockett at the Alamo."

Ross, Thom

Washington-based artist whose acrylic-on-paper Crockett and Alamo collection debuted at the Keene Gallery in San Antonio, Texas, on March 1, 1997. Among his original Crockett creations were *Davy Crockett and His Fiddle* and *Davy at the Doorway*. Ross later created the painting *Davy Crockett at the Alamo* for this author.

Rourke, Constance

Author of the 1934 book, *Davy Crockett.*

Royal Bengal Cigars

Early twentieth century cigar company which printed a "Men of History" card set that included a Davy Crockett card. The back of the card states: "At the batle of the Alamo he was one of six suvivors who . . . was treacherously executed by order of General Santa Anna."

Russell, George

Contemporary friend of Crockett's who is first mentioned in *A Narrative of the Life of David Crockett of the State of Tennessee* during a Creek Indian War scouting party episode. Although considered too young by Maj. John H. Gibson to accompany Crockett on the patrol, the famous frontiersman supported the young man by stating "that Russell could go as far as he could, and I must have him along."

Russel, George

Sidekick character played by Buddy Ebsen to Fess Parker's Davy Crockett in the Walt Disney 1954-1955 trilogy, *Davy Crockett, King of the Wild Frontier*. Russel appears with Crockett in all three episodes plus the two prequels, "Davy Crockett's Keelboat Race" and "Davy Crockett and the River Pirates." Ebsen recalled his Crockett experiences in his 1993 autobiography, *The Other Side of Oz.* In 1988, *The Magical World of Disney* revived the

Crockett series with Tim Dunigan starring as Crockett and Gary Grubbs playing Russel. The George Russel character also appears as a buckskinnned frontiersman played by Robert Weil during the SWAT-team shootout sequence in David Zucker's *Naked Gun 2½: The Smell of Fear* in 1991.

Saint Jean, Pierre
Nineteenth-century painter who created an 1828 portrait of Davy Crockett, which is now held in a private collection. A small reproduction of the image is featured in the *Encyclopedia Britannica* entry on "Davy Crockett."

St. George, Harry
Author of the 1879 "dime novel" *Daring Davy, the Young Bear Killer; or The Trail of the Border Wolf.*

Sally Ann Thunder and Whirlwind Crockett
Steven Kellogg's 1995 children's book which is based upon the fictitious character who "marries" the Davy Crockett character from the mid-nineteenth century Crockett Almanacs. Kellogg, who also ilustrated the book, based his story on several almanac tales, including "A Thief of an Alligator," "A Tongariferous Fight with an Alligator" and "Mike Fink Trying to Scare Mrs. Crockett."

Sanford, William R.
Co-author (with Carl R. Green) of the 1966 book *Davy Crockett; Defender of the Alamo.*

Santrey, Laurence
Author of the 1983 children's booklet *Davy Crockett: Young Pioneer.*

Schaare, C. R.
Author of the 1935 children's book *The Life of Davy Crockett in Picture and Story.*

Schneider, John
Actor who played Davy Crockett in the 1995 television movie *James A. Michener's "Texas."*

Sears, Alfred D.
Actor who played Davy Crockett in the 1916 motion picture *The Martyrs of the Alamo or The Birth of Texas.*

Shackford, James Atkins
Author of the comprehensive 1956 biography, *David Crockett, The Man and the Legend.* Due to illness, however, Shackford was unable to complete the work. His brother, John B. Shackford, ultimately edited the original manuscript into its "five movements" structure: "The Long Haul," "The Stiff Climb," "Up and Over," "Down and Under," and "Out." Noted Michael A. Lofaro in the 1986 University of North Carolina Press paperback edition introduction: "In the final analysis, James Atkins Shackford's ground-breaking achievement makes this biography the unequivocal starting point for everyone interested in the Crockett of history and legend."

Shapiro, Irwin
Author of the 1944 children's book *Yankee Thunder: The Legendary Life of Davy Crockett.* In 1955, Shapiro provided the text for several Walt Disney-authorized publications including the "Little Golden Book," *Walt Disney's Davy Crockett, King of the Wild Frontier, Davy Crockett's Keelboat Race,* and the *Davy Crockett Stamp Book.* Shapiro also wrote a chapter on Crockett in his 1958 book, *Tall Tales of America.*

Shegogue, James Hamilton
Nineteenth-century artist who created an 1831 watercolor on paper of David Crockett.

Silver Tomahawk
Ceremonial weapon presented to Crockett by the Young Whigs of Philaelphia in 1834. The tomahawk's left-face blade was inscribed with "Crockett." The anti-Andrew Jackson political group also presented a rifle to him which he christened "Pretty Betsey."

Singer, A. L.
Author of the 1991 children's books, *Davy Crockett and the Pirates of Cave-in Rock* and *Davy Crockett and the King of the River.*

Sioux Slaughter
One of David Thompson's paperback titles in his fictional "Davy Crockett" series. In *Sioux Slaughter* (1997), Crockett travels to the Great Plains where he confronts buffalo herds and Sioux warriors.

Sketches and Eccentricities of Colonel David Crockett of West Tennessee
Matthew St. Clair Clarke's 1833 book about Crockett (originally titled *A Narrative of the Life of David Crockett of West Tennessee*). Although Crockett dismissed this book he probably assisted in its creation.

Smith, Richard Penn
Ghostwriter of the 1836 publication *Col. Crockett's Exploits and Adventures in Texas . . . Written by Himself.*

Smith, Samuel D.
Author of *Historical Background and Archeological Testing of the Davy Crockett Birthplace State Historic Area, Greene County, Tennessee*, a 1980 publication of Division of Archeology, Tennessee Department of Conservation.

Sockdolager! A Tale of Davy Crockett in Which the Old Tennessee Bear Hunts Meets up With the Constitution of the United States
A 1961 reprint of Edward S. Ellis' 1884 book, *The Life of Colonel David Crockett.*

The Son of Davy Crockett
Title of 1941 B-Western starring William "Wild Bill" Elliott.

"Son of the West"
Nickname given to Crockett by Philadelphia publishers Carey and Hart in a February 7, 1834, commercial broadside ad-

vertising the forthcoming *Narrative of the Life of Col. David Crockett of Tennessee.*

Spielberg, Steven
Motion picture director who identifed Crockett's "Be sure you're right, and then go ahead" as the motto which governed his award-winning career. In an interview in *People* magazine (March 15-22, 1999), Spielberg said: "That was the Davy Crockett motto and I've lived by it all my life."

Sprague, William C.
Author of the 1915 biography *Davy Crockett.*

Star Trek: Deep Space Nine
Paramount Pictures' syndicated television show which occasionally featured dialogue about Davy Crockett delivered by some of its outer space characters. The inclusion of Crockett (and Alamo) lines began in 1998, thanks to the show's executive producer, Ira Steven Behr, a member of The Alamo Society.

Steele, William O.
Author of the 1956 children's book *Davy Crockett's Earthquake.*

Stephenson, Nathaniel W.
Author of the 1921 volume *Texas and the Mexican War,* which was part of Yale University Press' *The Chronicles of America* series. Stephenson admirably compared Crockett to "a Norse Viking in an Icelandic saga."

Story of David Crockett for Young Readers, The
Frances M. Perry's 1900 entry in the Baldwin's Biographical Booklet series. The author identifies Crockett as one of six Alamo defenders who were captured and brought before General Santa Anna: "The dauntless Crockett gave the spring of a tiger toward the dark leader, Santa Anna. But before he could reach him he had been cut down by a dozen swords."

Story of Davy Crockett, The
Jane Corby's 1922 children's book.

Story of Davy Crockett, The
Enid LaMonte Meadowcraft's 1952 children's book. The book, which is illustrated by Charles B. Falls, traces Crockett's life from his childhood to his final journey to the Alamo. The author makes no specific mention of Crockett's death; however, Meadowcraft states: "But when the attack ended, after an hour of bitter fighting, not one of them was left alive."

Story of Davy Crockett, The: Frontier Hero
Walter Retan's 1993 children's book. The author traces Crockett's life from his childhood in Tennessee to his final days at the Alamo in 1836. The book features the most awkwardly illustrated Alamo compound in print, an elongated stockade mission-fortress. Retan cites the conflicting accounts of Crockett's death in the "Davy's Last Stand" chapter.

Strong Springs
Later name of the area in Tennessee at the junction of the Nolichucky River and Limestone Creek where Crockett was born.

Sunrise in My Pocket or The Last Days of Davy Crockett
Edwin Justus Mayer's 1941 three-act play about "the last three months in the life of Davy Crockett."

Sutton, Felix
Author of the 1955 children's pamphlet, *The Picture Story of Davy Crockett.*

Taliaferro, Ernie
Actor who played the title role in the 1996 Steve Warren play, *The Confessions of David Crockett.*

"Talkin' with Fess"
A question and answer column in *The Alamo Journal* during the late 1980s and early 1990s written by Fess Parker, star of *Davy Crockett, King of the Wild Frontier.*

The Alamo Journal, April 1994, graphics by Phil Riordan.

Tall Tales of America

Irwin Shapiro's 1958 collection of early American frontier heroes, which features a chapter titled "Davy Crockett, the Yaller Blossum o' the Forest" in which the famous frontiersman battles a comet in a dance marathon!

Tall Tales of Davy Crockett, The

Facsimile edition (complete title: *The Tall Tales of Davy Crockett: The Second Nashville Series of Crockett Almanacs, 1839-1841*) of some of the most vivid Crockett almanacs. This 1987 publication features an excellent preface and Crockett chronology by Michael A. Lofaro. According to Lofaro, the Nashville series of almanacs (which were actually published in Boston): "was one of the most important forces in the development of the tall tale Crockett because it showcased him as the epitome of the boisterous backwoods hero. . . ."

Tallussahatchee

Massacre site of forty-six native American warriors by Crockett and his fellow soldiers on November 3, 1813, during the Creek Indian War. Noted Crockett in his autobiography: "The number that we took prisoners, being added to the number we killed, amounted to one hundred and eighty-six; though I don't remember the exact number of either. We had five of our men killed."

Taylor, Vincent Frank

Author of the 1955 book *David Crockett: The Bravest of Them All Who Died in the Alamo.*

Tennessee's Hero of the Alamo, Col. David Crockett, and Business Men's Directory

Lawrenceburg, Tennessee, publication from 1922 which featured the poem "Hymn of the Alamo" about Crockett and his fellow defenders.

Texas Adventure, The

An Encountarium™ F/X Theatre located in San Antonio, Texas, which featured a holographic Davy Crockett at the siege and Battle of the Alamo. The Texas Adventure™ opened in 1994 and its lobby included *Crockett's Last Stand,* the highly-detailed diorama created by Tom Feely.

Texas and the Mexican War

Nathaniel W. Stephenson's 1921 contribution to the multi-volume Yale University Press series *The Chronicles of America.* The author's devoted description of Crockett is practically unrivaled by any other author: "Crockett, the dead shot, setting down his rifle, and smiting with his bow the strings of his violin, while nearer and nearer crept the encircling host of enemies - is there any finer instance of that figure which romance loves, the warrior-minstrel of the forlorn hope!"

Texas Monthly

Austin-based periodical which featured a November 1986 cover story titled "Davy Crockett: Hero or Hype?" The front page stated: "Should we all still believe in a man who wasn't born on a mountaintop, hardly ever wore a coonskin cap, and surrendered at the Alamo?" The issue contained an article, "Davy Crockett, Still King of the Wild Frontier," written by Paul Andrew Hutton and an interview with Fess Parker conducted by Stephen Harrigan.

Texas Trailer, The; or, Davy Crockett's Last Bear Hunt

Beadle Boy's Library "dime novel" written by Edward S. Ellis under the pen name Charles E. LaSalle in 1886. Reprinted in 1878 as *Col. Crockett, the Texan Trailer.*

Texican Terror

One of David Thompson's paperback titles in his fictional "Davy Crockett" series. In *Texican Terror* (1998), Crockett travels to Spanish-controlled San Antonio where the famous Tennessean battles law-breaking "freebooters."

The Real . . . David Crockett, Authentic and Illustrated

Historical booklet written by Judge John Morrison and Col. Bob Hamsley in 1955 which celebrates the famous Tennessean and his home state. Of Crockett's death: "No one knows just how Colonel Crockett died at the Alamo, but his valor and courage give more credence to the tradition that he was one of six Americans who survived the assault . . . [and was subsequently executed].

Thirty-second Militia
Tennessee militia regiment of Franklin County in which Crockett was elected lieutenant on May 22, 1816.

Thompson, David
Author (real name: David Robbins) of the Davy Crockett historical fiction paperback series: *Homecoming* (1996), *Sioux Slaughter* (1997), *Blood Hunt* (1997), *Mississippi Mayhem* (1997), *Blood Rage* (1997), *Comanche Country* (1998), *Texican Terror* (1998), and *Cannibal Country* (1998).

Thompson, Ernest
Author of the 1956 booklet *The Fabulous David Crockett.*

Three Roads to the Alamo
William C. Davis' 1998 book which traces the lives of Crockett, James Bowie, and William B. Travis. Davis describes Crockett not as a Jacksonian era "common man," but as a "self-made man" with a "spirit of adventure." According to Davis: "He was the most famous man in the Alamo, yet his death was just like his birth, an event shrouded in complete obscurity." Of Crockett's death: "the nagging fact is that we will almost certainly never know for sure [how Crockett died]."

Timanus, Rod
Author of the 1999 book *On the Crockett Trail.*

Tocqueville, Alexis de
French writer who commented on Crockett during his 1831 sojourn in the United States and published *Democracy in the United States* in 1835. Of Crockett: "He has no education, can read with difficulty, has no property, no fixed residence, but passes his life hunting, selling his game to live, and dwelling continuously in the woods."

Tolliver, Arthur
Author of the 1944 children's book *The Wild Adventures of Davy Crockett: Based Mainly on the Writings of the Hero of the Alamo.*

Tousey, Sanford
Author of the 1948 children's book *Davy Crockett, Hero of the Alamo.*

Townsend, Tom
Author of the 1987 children's book, *Davy Crockett: An American Hero.*

Trotman, Felicity
Co-author (with Shirley Greenway) of the 1986 children's book, *Davy Crockett.*

Turner, Frederick Jackson
Famous historian who delivered the epic presentation "the Significance of the Frontier in American History" at the 1893 World's Congress of Historians and Historical Students in Chicago, and authored *The Frontier in American History,* a 1920 republication of previously published essays about the American frontier. In his chapter on "The Old West," Turner commented on the mid-eighteenth century westward movement of settlers which included "the ancestors of John C. Calhoun, Abraham Lincoln, Jefferson Davis, Stonewall Jackson, James K. Polk, Sam Houston, and Davy Crockett. . . ."

United States Hotel
Crockett's favorite hotel in Philadelphia, Pennsylvania. He stayed at the Chestnut Street hotel on two separate occasions in 1834.

Von Schmidt, Eric
Artist who created the 1986 painting *Davy and the Bear*

which was featured for the first time in print in Gary Foreman's *Crockett: The Gentleman from the Cane*.

Voss, Frederick S.

Co-author (with James C. Kelly) of the 1986 Tennessee State Museum booklet *Davy Crockett, Gentleman From The Cane*.

Wade, Mary Dodson

Author of the 1992 children's book, *David Crockett—Sure He Was Right*.

Warren, Charles Dudley

Author of the 1888 "dime novel" *Killb'ar, the Guide, or, Davy Crockett's Crooked Trail*. Reprinted in 1888 as *Rocky Rover Kit, or Davy Crockett's Crooked Trail*.

Walt Disney's Davy Crockett, King of the Wild Frontier

Irwin Shapiro's 1955 children's title in Simon and Schuster's "Little Golden Book" series. Although this book was based on the popular Disney television series, it devotes several pages to such legendary tales as Crockett "riding a streak of lightning" and "catching a comet by the tail." Crockett is seen in the Mel Crawford-created art fighting at the Alamo but the page text simply states that "He helped fight a great battle at the Alamo."

Washington, George

First president of the United States whose image was featured on a cameo pin which Crockett wore during a rifle shoot in Jersey City, New Jersey, in 1834.

Waters, Sterling

Actor who played Davy Crockett in the 1938 motion picture *The Alamo: "Shrine of Texas Liberty."*

Wave High the Banner: A Novel Based on the Life of Davy Crockett

Dee Brown's 1942 book. Of Crockett's death: "But the shining bayonets were coming over the barricade now, stabbing, slashing, and a man must fight, a man must. . . ." The book was most recently reprinted in 1999 with an introduction by Paul Andrew Hutton and new cover art by Michael Schreck.

Wayne, John
Legendary actor who played Davy Crockett in the 1960 motion picture *The Alamo*. Wayne also produced and directed the film, which was nominated for a Best Picture Oscar©. In 1999, the Franklin Mint issued a small "John Wayne" Davy Crockett figure.

Webb, Noel
Actor who portrays the holographic Davy Crockett at The Texas Adventure™ in San Antonio, Texas.

"We Didn't Start the Fire"
Billy Joel's 1990 single which pays homage to United States history since the end of World War II, and acknowledges the Crockett craze during the mid-1950s with the lyrical line: "Davy Crockett, Peter Pan, Elvis Presley, Disneyland."

"When Davy Crockett Met the San Antonio Rose"
Red River Dave's 1955 Decca Records single which features Crockett's actual fiddle. The label credits The Witte Memorial Museum in San Antonio, which held the instrument.

The Wild Adventures of Davy Crockett: Based mainly on the writings of the Hero of the Alamo
Arthur Tolliver's 1944 children's book.

Wildfire, Nimrod
Fictitious frontier character created by James Kirke Paulding for his 1831 play *The Lion of the West* and associated with David Crockett. Actor James Hackett originally played the Crockett-like figure.

Willet, Edward
Author of the 1908 "dime novel" *Davy Crockett's Boy Hunter.*

Wilson, Abraham
Tennessee merchant who David worked for during a six-month period in 1802 in order to pay of his father's $36 debt.

Wilson, Nat
Author of the 1955 "Triple Nickel Book," *Davy Crockett: Danger From the Mountain.*

Winchester, Marcas
Friend of Crockett's who helped finance the frontiersman's political career in the 1820s.

Winningham, Geoff
Voice-over cast member who portrayed Davy Crockett in *The Death of Davy Crockett,* a 1993 video documentary created by Brian Huberman.

With Crockett and Bowie, or Fighting for the Lone-Star Flag
Kirk Munroe's 1905 children's book.

Witte Museum
San Antonio, Texas, museum which showcased a "Remembering The Alamo" exhibit in 1986, and culminated with a "Davy Crockett Birthday Party" on August 17, 1986. The Witte Museum showed a copy of *Davy Crockett, King of the Wild Frontier* on a large screen while birthday cake was served. In addition, an on-site living history program was organized by Gary Foreman Productions.

Wright, David
Well-known frontier artist who created *Crossroads to Destiny* in 1999. The painting depicts Crockett in 1813 during the Creek Indian War.

Yankee Thunder: The Legendary Life of Davy Crockett
Irwin Shapiro's 1944 children's book.

Young Davy Crockett, or, The Hero of Silver Gulch

A 1917 "dime novel" in the Pluck and Luck "Old Scout" series.

Young, Richard

Actor who played Davy Crockett in the 1985 *Amazing Stories* television episode "Alamo Jobe."

Zucker, David

California-based motion picture director-producer-writer, and Davy Crockett memorabilia collector who has included a number of Crockett touches in his films, including the *Naked Gun* series, *High School High,* and *BASEketball.* Zucker, who purchased gunsmith Houston Harrison's replication of one of Crockett's early rifles in 1989, has hosted a series of "Davy Crockett Rifle Frolics" at his California ranch. Zucker even portrayed the buckskin frontiersman in a SWAT-team shoot out scene in *Naked Gun 2½: The Smell of Fear.*

Colonel Crockett and the great bear skin
Crockett Almanack image courtesy of Gary Foreman

DAVID CROCKETT
NUMBERS

"David Crockett" painting by Charles B. Normann.
—Courtesy of Texas State Library & Archives Commission

DAVY CROCKETT NUMBERS

1	Highest position reached on the *Billboard* chart for "The Ballad of Davy Crockett" sung by Bill Hayes in 1955.
2	# of wives.
3	# of terms served in the U.S. House of Representatives.
4	# of members in "Crockett's Company" in *Davy Crockett, King of the Wild Frontier.*
5	# of Walt Disney-produced televison episodes of *Davy Crockett, King of the Wild Frontier* in 1954 and 1955.
6	# of months Crockett spent in school.
7	# of inches in length of the "Crockett" cigar made by the Finck Cigar Company.
8	# of brothers and sisters.
10	# of gallons of whiskey acquired by Crockett in exchange for his labor on a river boat in early 1822.
12	# of classrooms in the Crockett Elementary School built in Lawrenceburg, Tennesee, in 1951.
20	# of acres received in Lawrence County for his participation in the Creek Indian War (as part of the War of 1812).
22	# of cities on Fess Parker's 1955 *Davy Crockett, King of the Wild Frontier* promotional tour.
24	# of dollars paid to the estate of David Crockett for his service in the Texas Revolution.
25	# of dollars fined for missing jury duty in 1824.

29	# of verses of "The Ballad of Davy Crockett" (9 more than printed in the sheet music) sung on the three-part *Disneyland* television series.
35	# of grandchildren.
49	# of years old at the time of his death at the Alamo.
60	# of dollars paid by Thomas J. Rusk, secretary of war for Texas, to Crockett for two rifles in 1836.
97	# of days served as a soldier in the Creek Indian War in 1813.
105	# of bears allegedly killed in one winter.
65.59	# of dollars and cents actually payed for service in the Creek Indian War.
65.65	# of dollars and cents owed for service in the Creek Indian War.
80	# of bubble gum cards in each of the two Topps "Davy Crockett" sets printed in 1956.
120	# of packs of one-cent "Davy Crockett" bubble gum cards per Topps Bubble Gum Card boxes in 1956.
186	# of dollars pickpocketed from Crockett's wallet in Camden, New Jersey, in 1834.
200	# of Mexican soldiers killed by Crockett during the siege and Battle of the Alamo according to the 1989 textbook *A Proud Nation*.
240	# of dollars awarded to Robert Patton Crockett for the loss of his father's property during the siege and Battle of the Alamo.
500	# of dollars per week Fess Parker earned for playing *Davy Crockett, King of the Wild Frontier*.
1,265	# of seats in the Crockett Theatre, which opened in 1950 in Lawrenceburg, Tennessee.
1,280	# of Texas acres awarded to Crockett's widow, Elizabeth, for his service in the Texas Revolution.
1618	# of the Lawrenceburg, Tennessee, David Crockett Post of the Veterans of Foreign War, which was chartered on June 5, 1938.
1,679	# of tons in weight of the clipper ship *David Crockett*.

2,599	# of votes received in losing the congressional election of 1825 (his opponent Col. Adam Alexander received 2,866).
3,985	# of votes received in winning the congressional election of 1833 (his opponent William Fitzgerald received 3,812).
4,400	# of votes received in losing the congressional election in 1835 (his opponent Adam Huntsman received 4,652 votes).
5,000	Approximate number of different commercial items produced by manufacturers during the Davy Crockett Craze of the mid-1950s.
5,868	# of votes received in winning the congressional election of 1827 (his nearest opponent, Col. Adam Alexander received 3,646 votes).
6,773	# of votes received in winning the congressional election of 1829 (his nearest opponent, Col. Adam Alexander received 3,641 votes).
7,948	# of votes received in losing the congressional election of 1831 (his opponent William Fitzgerald received 8,534 votes).
94,800	# of dollars spent by the George Greenman Company to build the clipper ship *David Crockett*.
750,000	# of Davy Crockett record albums sold by Walt Disney.
10,000,000	# of copies of "The Ballad of Davy Crockett" sold by various artists according to Walt Disney by 1963.
120,000,000	# of 5-cent Davy Crockett stamps initially issued by the United States Post Office in 1967.

THE
TEXAS MAGAZINE

Vol. I.   DECEMBER, 1896.   No. 8.

PEN SKETCH BY WM. P. FORD.

DAVY CROCKETT.

PUBLISHED MONTHLY AT AUSTIN, TEXAS.

ILLUSTRATED.

PER YEAR, $1.   PER COPY, 10c.

"Davy Crockett sketch by William P. Ford."
— Courtesy Texas State Library & Archives Commission

CROCKETT
LISTS

TOP TEN DAVY CROCKETT BOOKS

Here's an alphabetically-arranged roster of the best Davy Crockett books. These titles are essential to any library dedicated to the "King of the Wild Frontier."

A Narrative of the Life of David Crockett of the State of Tennessee
David Crockett
1834
(1973 Tennesseana Edition)
This facsimile edition features excellent annotations by James Atkins Shackford and Stanley J. Folmsbee that allow readers to more fully understand the language, chronology, and background behind Crockett's lively autobiography.

Crockett at Two Hundred: New Persepctives on the Man and the Myth
Michael A. Lofaro and Joe Cummings, editors
1989
A fine collection of essays including "Davy Crockett: An Exposition on Hero Worship," "David Crockett and the Rhetoric of Tennessee Politics," and "Davy Crockett and the Tradition of the Westerner in American Cinema."

Crockett: The Gentleman from the Cane
Gary Foreman
1986
This glossy publication is rich in photographs, art, and related images of the David Crockett of history and the Davy Crockett of legend. Foreman provides a visual appreciation of the early trans-Appalachian frontier that other Crockett titles lack.

David Crockett: The Man and the Legend
James Atkins Shackford
1956
This scholarly book is replete with Crockett letters, extensive notes, and contemporary data. Shackford's work is comprehensive, thorough, and rich in information.

Davy Crockett: Gentleman From the Cane
James Kelly and Frederick S. Voss
1986
A richly illustrated publication which accompanied a 1986 "Exhibition Commemorating Crockett's Life and Legend on the 200th Anniversary of His Birth" at the Tennessee State Museum in Nashville. The graphic presentation of various Crockett portraits, documents, and memorabilia is first rate.

Davy Crockett: The Man, The Legend, The Legacy, 1786-1986
Michael A. Lofaro, editor
1985
The title says it all. This is arguably the best single reference work on the Crockett of history and popular culture. Great essays on everything from the Crockett almanacs and "Davy Crockett in Theater" to songs, movies, and folklore.

Defense of a Legend: Crockett and the de la Peña Diary
Bill Groneman
1994
This book raises questions about the suggestion that Crockett was executed following his surrender at the Alamo. Groneman identifies and explains inconsistencies in the papers of José Enrique de la Peña which form the foundation of the Crockett execution theory.

How Did Davy Die?
Dan Kilgore
1978
This forty-eight-page book supports the account of Mexican officer José Enrique de la Peña, who stated that Crockett was executed after the Battle of the Alamo. Kilgore supports de la

Peña's observations about Crockett's final moments with other contemporary accounts.

The Davy Crockett Craze
Paul F. Anderson
1996
A glossy, fun-filled pictoral study of the Walt Disney-inspired Davy Crockett Craze of 1954-1956. Anderson combines history, film production notes, and commercialism in a thoughtful and nostalgic volume.

Three Roads to the Alamo
William C. Davis
1998
This is the best biography of Crockett since Shackford's 1956 classic. Davis, a prolific Civil War author, features Crockett (along with James Bowie and William B. Travis) in this mammoth work that is augmented by comprehensive notes.

TOP DOZEN
DAVY CROCKETT BOOKS FOR KIDS

Here are the best children's books about the famous Tennessee frontiersman and Alamo hero. And nearly every one of the chronologically-arranged titles is richly illustrated.

Davy Crockett's Boy Hunter
Edward Willett
1908
Twenty-three chapters of tall tales from the popular Beadles Frontier Series.

The Story of Davy Crockett
Enid Lamonte Meadowcraft
1952

Meadowcraft's thoughtful 178-page treatment of Crockett's life is augmented by C.B. Falls' pen and ink illustrations.

Legends of Davy Crockett
Ardis Edwards Burton
1955
Burton adapted this Walt Disney-authorized book from Tom Blackburn's 1954-1955 teleplays, which include the post-Alamo "River Pirates" prequel. Many of illustrator Michael Arens' vivid images are inspired by scenes from the original TV episodes. And this book remains a desired collectible among baby boomers.

Davy Crockett: American Hero
Bruce Grant
1955
Colorful drawings by William Timmins make this one of the best Crockett books for the youngest of readers.

The Picture Story of Davy Crockett
Felix Hutton
1955
This book, which is wonderfully illustrated by H. B. Vestal, covers Crockett's life from his childhood to his defense of the Alamo.

Walt Disney's Davy Crockett, King of the Wild Frontier
Irwin Shapiro
1955
This "Little Golden Book" is the best seller of all the mid-1950s Crockett titles. Mel Crawford's artwork visually traces Crockett's life past the Alamo into the realm of legendary folk-lore.

Davy Crockett, Young Pioneer
Laurence Santrey
1983
This delightful booklet concentrates on Crockett's young days. Santrey, though, has Davy dying one day too soon at the

Alamo. Francis Livingston's sketches are quite effective, especially her final drawing on page forty-eight.

Davy Crockett: An American Hero
Tom Townsend
1987
The author's historical story is strengthened by his use of information from Crockett's 1834 autobiography and other useful secondary texts.

Davy Crockett at the Alamo
Justine Korman
1991
This title is the fourth in Disney's "American Frontier" series. Based on the 1955 TV episode of the same name, *Davy Crockett at the Alamo* features illustrations by Charlie Shaw and a splendid color cover created by Mike Wepplo.

Davy Crockett: Hero of the Wild Frontier
Elizabeth R. Mosely
1991
Readers are introduced to Crockett at age nine in this book, and follow him until his death at the Alamo. Top notch art work by Thomas Beecham.

Sally Ann Thunder Ann Whirlwind Crockett
Steven Kellogg
1995
A visual tale based on the mid-nineteenth century Crockett Almanacs. It describes the larger-than-life female frontier character who "weds" Davy Crockett. Kellogg also provided the engaging illustrations.

A Picture Book of Davy Crockett
David A. Adler
1996
This book is pure fun thanks to a spirited story along with John and Alexandra Wallner's cheerful illustrations.

TOP 10 QUESTIONS/COMMENTS ASKED ABOUT DAVID CROCKETT AT THE ALAMO*

David Crockett fought and died at the Battle of the Alamo in 1836. The Alamo, located in San Antonio, Texas, is visited by millions of tourists each year. Dorothy Black, a member of the Daughters of the Republic of Texas, worked for many years at the Alamo church's information desk. She provided the following questions and comments that people regularly asked and posed about the famous Alamo defender. Dorothy Black offers a few responses to some of the frequently-asked questions. Items number three and number eight are the direct comments of Dorothy Black [DB]. Other questions are answered by William R. Chemerka [WRC].

1. Why isn't Crockett's name listed on the alphabetical wall plaques?
[DB: "Crockett, Bowie, Travis, and Bonham are located on 'The Commanders' Plaque.'"]

2. Where is Crockett's rifle, "Old Betsy?"
[WRC: "Crockett's 'Pretty Betsey' is privately owned by a family in the Northeast and is not currently on public display. Another rifle, sometimes called 'Betsey,' is in the collection of the Museum of East Tennessee History in Knoxville."]

3. People are curious about the custom regarding the snippet of his hair in the locket.

4. "How old was David Crockett when he died at the Alamo?"
[WRC: "Crockett was forty-nine years old on March 6, 1836. He would have been fifty years old on August 17, 1836."]

5. "Why was he here?"
[WRC: "He was a participant in Texas' revolution against Mexico."]

6. "Why is his buckskin vest so small?"
[WRC: "According to the Alamo Society's Dr. Todd Har-

burn, who created an exact copy of the vest several years ago, the original item reflects Crockett's chest size and the tight-fitting style of the period."]

7. "Where is his coonskin cap?"

[WRC: "Unknown. After the fall of the Alamo, Mrs. Dickinson stated that she saw Crockett's body and remembered 'seeing his peculiar cap lying by his side.'"]

8. People don't recognize his bronze bust and ask, "who is it?"

9. "Did Daniel Boone die here?"

[DB: "No. They confuse him with Crockett."]

10. "Where and how did David Crockett die?"

[WRC: "Although entire books have been written on this controversial question, there is no definitive answer as to the exact place and details of Crockett's death."]

* An exclusive entry for *The Davy Crockett Almanac & Book of Lists*.

TOP 10 MOST FREQUENTLY ASKED QUESTIONS AT THE CROCKETT TAVERN MUSEUM*

For years, Tim McCurry served as the tour guide at the Crockett Tavern Museum in Morristown, Tennessee. Although not related to David Crockett, McCurry maintains a "friend" membership in the Direct Descendants of David Crockett. He provided this list of the most frequently asked questions and answers.

1. How old was David Crockett when he died?

answer: Crockett was forty-nine years old when he died. He would have turned fifty years old on August 17, 1836.

2. Where is David Crockett buried?

answer: There is no grave of David Crockett. All the remains of the Alamo defenders were burned in funeral pyres following the March 6, 1836, battle.

3. Are there any descendants of David Crockett still living?

answer: Yes. There are more than 300 living descendants "officially" organized into the Direct Descendants of David Crockett.

4. Does any artifact at the Crockett Tavern Museum belong to the Crockett family?

answer: Yes. There are three artifacts which belonged to the Crockett family. One Tavern Museum log came from David Crockett's birth home; an old mill stone that rests outside the Tavern Museum belonged to John Crockett, David's father; and remnants of the well where the Crockett family received their water remain at the Tavern Museum.

5. When did David Crockett live at the Crockett Tavern?

answer: David Crockett lived at the tavern between November 1795 and August 1806 when he met and married Polly Finley.

6. How old was David Crockett when he married Polly Finley?

answer: David Crockett married Polly just before his twentieth birthday.

7. Did David Crockett really kill a bear when he was only three years old?

answer: No. This myth came from a line in the the popular song "The Ballad of Davy Crockett." However, David Crockett did kill 105 black bears in nine months when he was an adult.

8. Where is the "tavern" portion of the house? Where was whiskey served?

answer: The entire building is the tavern. Taverns in East Tennessee functioned much like a modern bed and breakfast inn. There was no bar where whiskey was served.

9. Was the land around the Tavern wilderness when the Crockett's moved to Morristown, Tennessee?

answer: Although Morristown did not exist, there were three thriving communities in the area. David Crockett first attempted to go to school six miles from the tavern in Russellville, Tennessee. An adjoining community called Whitesburg also existed. And Panther Creek, fifteen miles to the southwest of the Tavern, is where young David Crockett worked off one of his father's debts that the elder Crockett owed to a Quaker named John Canady.

10. How many children did David Crockett have?

answer: There were six children born to David Crockett and his two wives. His first wife, Polly, gave birth to John Wesley, William, and Margaret. David remarried a widow, Elizabeth Patton, who had two children. Following her marriage to David, Elizabeth gave birth to Robert Patton, Rebecca Elvira, and Matilda. David treated Elizabeth's first two children, George and Margaret Ann, as if they were his own.

* An exclusive entry for *The Davy Crockett Almanac & Book of Lists*.

BEST CROCKETT ALMANAC TITLES

The Davy Crockett Almanacs were printed from 1835 until 1856 by various publishers around the United States. Filled with tall tales, backwoods humor, entertaining illustrations, and practical information, these popular publications kept the spirit and legend of Davy Crockett alive with equally lively (and, sometimes, lengthy) titles.

Some almanac title pages featured slogans like the familiar "I leave this rule for others when I'm dead, be always sure you're right, then go ahead." Others featured such fanciful and comical expressions as "Crockett scared by an Owl," "Crockett's Method of Wading the Mississippi," and "Crockett's wonderful escape up Niagara Falls, on his Pet Alligator."

Here's a list of the best five Davy Crockett Almanac titles (arranged chronologically):

1. *Davy Crockett's Almanack, of Wild Sports of the West, and Life in the Backwoods. Calculated for all the States in the Union.* (1835)

2. *Crockett Yaller Flower Almanac. Go Ahead! Snooks, no danger her going off! The Ringtail Roarer! Ripsnorter! Circumflustercated Grinner's Guide!* (1836)

3. *Crockett's Awlmanaxe for 1839.* (1839)

4. *The Crockett Almanac. Containing Adventures, Exploits, Sprees & Scrapes in the West, & Life and Manners in the Backwoods.* (1839)

5. *Ben Hardin's Crockett Almanac. With Correct Astronomical Calculations; For each State in the Union—territories and Canada. Rows—Sprees and Scrapes in the West: Life and Manners in the Backwoods: and Terrible Adventures on the Ocean.* (1842)

CROCKETT'S CONGRESSIONAL PEERS FROM TENNESSEE

The Honorable David Crockett served three terms in the United States House of Representatives. He was elected as a member of the Democratic Party to the 20th Congress (1827-1829) and the 21st Congress (1829-1831). Crockett was elected as a member of the Whig Party to the 23rd Congreess (1833-1835).

Here's a roster of his fellow Tennesseans who served with him:

20th Congress
John Bell
John Blair
Robert Desha
Jacob C. Isacks
Pryor Lea
John H. Marable
James C. Mitchell
James K. Polk

21st Congress
John Bell
John Blair
Robert Desha
Jacob C. Isacks
Cave Johnson
Pryor Lea
James K. Polk
James Standifer

23rd Congress
John Bell
John Blair
Samuel Bunch
David W. Dickinson
William C. Dunlap
John B. Forster
William M. Inge
Cave Johnson
Luke Lea
Balie Peyton
James K. Polk
James Standifer

DAVY CROCKETT'S
FIRST RAILROAD JOURNEY*

Crockett took his first trip on a railroad on April 29, 1834, during his Whig-promoted tour of the Northeast. Crockett left Philadelphia and crossed New Jersey toward New York harbor, aboard a passenger car on the relatively new Camden and Amboy Railroad, which was the first steam-powered passenger rail system built in the Garden State. At the time, the Camden and Amboy Railroad was the fastest transportation link between Philadelphia and New York City. Crockett departed Philadelphia on April 29, and sailed up the Delaware River on the vessel *New Philadelphia* to nearby Camden City, New Jersey. At Camden City, he boarded the Camden and Amboy Raiload for the journey to South Amboy, which was located next to Raritan Bay across from Staten Island and Manhattan. Crockett was the second celebrity to travel the railroad. Earlier, Madam Murat, wife of Prince Murat, a nephew of the late Napoleon Bonaparte, who was residing in Bordentown, New Jersey, at the time, was the first woman to ride the railroad.

Here is a list of the New Jersey communities and towns that Crockett traveled through in 1834 on his Camden and Amboy Railroad trip:

Camden City	Yardville
Fish House	Hightstown
Beverly	Cranberry
Burlington City	Prospect Plains
Florence	Jamesburg
Kinkora	Spottswood
White Hall (White Hill)	Old Bridge
Bordentown	South Amboy

* An exclusive for *The Davy Crockett Almanac & Book of Lists*.

"David Crockett—Pioneer Soldier and Statesman."
— Courtesy Texas State Library and Archives Commission

AUTHOR COMMENTS
ABOUT DAVID CROCKETT

Walter Blair
   Davy Crockett; Legendary Frontier Hero (1955)
   ". . . a very interesting and likable fellow."

William C. Davis
   Three Roads to the Alamo (1998)
   ". . . an original, perhaps, but not a gentleman in the eyes
of America. . . ."

Mark Derr
   *The Frontiersman; The Real Life and Many Legends of Davy
Crockett* (1993)
   ". . . [a] common man, eccentric, independent."

Richard M. Dorson
   Davy Crockett: American Comic Legend (1939)
   ". . . an immortal part of the national mythology, secure of
a place in the American pantheon."

Gary Foreman
   Crockett: The Gentleman from the Cane (1986)
   ". . . an intelligent, witty man who possessed an unusual
amount of physical strength, humor, and above all, independence."

Bill Groneman
   Defense of a Legend; Crockett and the de la Peña Diary (1994)
   ". . . the very model of the trans-Appalachian frontiersman. . . ."

Paul Andrew Hutton
   introduction to *A Narrative of the Life of David Crockett* (1987)
   ". . . an extraordinary man."

Dan Kilgore
How Did Davy Die? (1978)
". . . one of America's greatest folk heroes."

Walter Lord
A Time to Stand (1961)
". . . a political natural on the frontier."

Enid LaMonte Meadowcraft
The Story of Davy Crockett (1952)
". . . a true American."

James A. Michener
Texas (1985)
". . . a famous raconteur whose disreputable stories narrated in dialect often made him look ridiculous."

Constance Rourke
Davy Crockett (1934)
". . . a man of statue with a significant career."

Laurence Santrey
Davy Crockett; Young Pioneer (1983)
". . . a man in his own right, and a very able one, too."

James Atkins Shackford
David Crockett; The Man and the Legend (1956)
". . . the essence of the backwoods."

V. F. Taylor
David Crockett (1955)
"The bravest of them all who died at the Alamo."

David Thompson
Homecoming (1996)
". . . the muscular frontiersman."

Lon Tinkle
13 Days to Glory; The Siege of the Alamo (1958)

". . . the flavor of frontier life."

Dale L. Walker
  (1997)
  ". . . a beloved national personality long before he ventured to Texas."

DAVY CROCKETT IN THE MOVIES

Davy Crockett—In Hearts United (1909)
  Charles K. French stars in this New York Motion Picture Company's silent film based on the Frank Hitchcok play *Davy Crockett, Or Be Sure You're Right, Then Go Ahead.*

Davy Crockett (1910)
  Sewlig Polyscope Company's silent film. No cast list was made—even the actor who plays the celebrated title character remains unknown.

The Immortal Alamo (1911)
  Gaston Melies-produced silent film. Francis Ford is some-times identified as Crockett in this motion picture, but recent research by film historian Frank Thompson suggests that the actor did not portray the famous Alamo defender; as a matter of fact, the Crockett character is not clearly identifiable in the film.

Martyrs of the Alamo (1915)
  Alfred D. Sears stars as Crockett in this D. W. Griffith-super-vised Fine Arts Company silent film.

Davy Crockett Up To Date (1915)
  United Film Service's slapstick comedy about the famous frontiersman, according to essayist William Eric Jamborsky in *Crockett at Two Hundred; New Perspectives on the Man and the Myth.*

However, according to film historian Frank Thompson, there is no record of such a film ever being made.

Davy Crockett (1916)
Dustin Farnum stars in the title role in this Oliver Morosco Photoplay Company silent film.

Davy Crockett at the Fall of the Alamo (1926)
Cullen Landis stars in the title role in this first Crockett feature silent film.

Heroes of the Alamo (1937)
Lane Chandler stars as Crockett in this Henry Fraser-directed film. *Heroes of the Alamo* is the first film in which Crockett speaks.

The Alamo, "Shrine of Texas Liberty" (1938)
Sterling Waters stars as Crockett in this narrated black and white two-reeler.

Davy Crockett—Indian Scout (1950)
George Montgomery plays the title role (the Phoenix Films pressbook calls Montgomery's character "a cousin of the Davy Crockett of Alamo fame") in this cowboys and Indians shoot 'em up production.

Man From the Alamo (1953)
Trevor Bardette portrays an older Crockett in this Universal release, which stars Glenn Ford.

Davy Crockett, King of the Wild Frontier (1955)
Fess Parker stars in the title role in this Disney production which was edited from the three 1954-1955 televison episodes. Parker's outstanding characterization is still the one all other celluloid Crocketts are compared to.

The Last Command (1955)
Arthur Hunnicutt stars as a rough-edged Crockett in this Republic Pictures release.

Davy Crockett and the River Pirates (1956)

Fess Parker stars in the title role of this Disney production, which was edited from two 1955 TV episodes: "Davy Crockett's Keelboat Race" and "Davy Crockett and the River Pirates."

The First Texan (1956)

James Griffith portrays Crockett in this Byron Haskin-directed CinemaScope feature about Sam Houston, "the first Texan," played by Joel McCrea.

Alias Jesse James (1959)

Fess Parker makes a cameo appearance as Davy Crockett in this western comedy starring Bob Hope.

The Alamo (1960)

John Wayne stars as Crockett in the epic United Artists film that was nominated for seven Academy Awards.™ *The Alamo*, which was also directed by Wayne, won only one Oscar,™ for sound.

Houston: The Legend of Texas (1986)

Guy Arnold, an un-billed extra, portrays Crockett's lifeless body (face down, no less!) during a brief Battle of the Alamo aftermath sequence. This TV movie was released as a videocassette under the title *Gone to Texas*.

The Alamo: 13 Days to Glory (1987)

Brian Keith stars as Crockett in this Burt Kennedy-directed TV movie.

Alamo . . . The Price of Freedom (1988)

Merrill Connally, brother of the late Texas Governor John Connally, stars as an older Crockett in this giant-screen IMAX film. However, David Kanawah, takes over for Connally in the final battle scene sequence, and stunt team member William Chemerka doubles for the actor in the Alamo church explosion scene.

Naked Gun 2½: The Smell of Fear (1991)

Director David Zucker appears as Crockett in a cameo role during a modern SWAT-team shootout sequence in which two buckskin-clad frontiersmen (Zucker's Crockett and Robert Weil's "George Russel") join a squad of semiautomatic-shooting officers.

James A. Michener's "Texas" (1995)

John Schneider plays Crockett in this two-part TV movie. Originally released as a videocassette in 1994, this production was based upon the famous James A. Michener novel.

FESS PARKER'S TOP 10 MOST MEMORABLE SCENES FROM *DAVY CROCKETT, KING OF THE WILD FRONTIER**

Fess Parker starred as Davy Crockett in Walt Disney's 1954-1955 TV trilogy: "Davy Crockett, Indian Fighter," "Davy Crockett Goes to Congress," and "Davy Crockett at the Alamo." The three episodes were later edited and released as a motion picture in 1955 titled *Davy Crockett, King of the Wild Frontier.*

Here are Fess Parker's recollections about his most memorable scenes:

"Davy Crockett, Indian Fighter"
1. **"Grinning Down Redstick"**

"The final fight I had with Pat Hogan, who played the Creek chief, Red Stick, stands out in my mind. I thought that the scene in which he has me pinned up against a tree and I give him the grin was one of the silliest things I ever did on camera. But it seemed to work out all right."

2. "The Dangerous Bridge"

"Another memorable scene is one that features me and Buddy Ebsen, who played my companion, George Russel, leaving camp to go home. As a matter of fact, Buddy has recalled that scene as his scariest scene in the entire series. We had to cross a high wooden bridge without guard rails and ride towards a cannon crew, and we were rather high up. Buddy was trying to control his horse while he held on to a guitar! It was kind of funny."

3. "Arrow Ambush"

"In the ambush scene, I remember being shot by an Indian with a rubber-tipped arrow which hit me right above my left eyebrow, just missing my eye by about a half inch."

"Davy Crockett Goes To Congress"
1. "House of Representatives Speech"

"The speech. Crockett's inaugural 'half-horse, half-alligator' speech in Congress was a scene that I always will remember."

2. "Death of Polly Crockett"

"The scene in which I received the letter telling me that my wife, Polly, died was a difficult one to do. I actually based my reaction somewhat subsconsciously on how Gary Copper, playing Lou Gehrig, handled the ending scene of *Pride of the Yankees*. In that film, Cooper just turned and walked toward the dugout. I essentially did the same thing, and the director, Norman Foster, fortunately bought my interpretation of how to do it."

3. "General Jackson at Home"

"Working with Basil Ruysdael, who played Andrew Jackson, at Jackson's actual home, the Hermitage in Tennessee, was memorable. And the confrontation scene with William Bakewell, who played Major Norton as a lobbyist, was an exciting scene to be a part of."

"Davy Crockett at the Alamo"
1. "Farewell"

"The singing of 'Farewell' by Crockett and the men of the Alamo on the night before the final battle is a scene that immediately comes to mind. It was a poignant moment for those men who were about to die. I think the scene was well done."

2. "Drawing the Line"

"The drawing of the line in the dirt by Colonel Travis [played by Don Megowan] was an important moment. It was a fateful decision by those who crossed it."

3. "Death of Bowie"

"The death of Jim Bowie [played by Kenneth Tobey] was a very powerful scene that demonstrated the courage of his character."

4. "Crockett's Death"

"That was a difficult scene to do, with all the stuntmen and everything. But it was handled well by Mr. Disney. For me, well, it was the end!"

* An exclusive for *The Davy Crockett Almanac & Book of Lists*.

DAVID ZUCKER'S CROCKETT TOUCHES IN HIS FILMS*

David Zucker is an accomplished motion picture director/ producer (*Airplane!*, *Ruthless People*, the *Naked Gun* films, etc.) and collector of important historic Davy Crockett memorabilia. He has embellished several of his films with Davy Crockett touches.

The Naked Gun: From the Files of Police Squad (1989)

Lt. Frank Drebin, played by Leslie Nielsen, has an apartment that is decorated with framed Crockett portrait prints. In addition, a coonskin cap and a fringed buckskin jacket hang from a wall rack near his apartment's door.

The Naked Gun 2½: The Smell of Fear (1991)

The film's opening White House sequence features a life-size reproduction of John G. Chapman's 1834 portrait of Crockett hanging from a dining room wall. Director David Zucker dresses up like Crockett for a cameo appearance during a SWAT-team shoot out sequence. In the scene, Zucker is joined by California artist Robert Weil who plays George Russel.

Naked Gun 33 1/3: The Final Insult (1994)

Besides the obligatory coonskin cap that hangs from Lt. Frank Drebin's apartment wall are Crockett portrait prints by such nineteenth century artists as John G. Chapman, James H. Shegogue, and John Naegle.

High School High (1996)

Idealistic teacher John Lovitz departs from the Wellington School, a high-class, private educational institution that features a life-size John G. Chapman portrait of Crockett. The painting's brass identification plate states "Class of 1836," the year Crockett died at the Alamo. In addition, the portrait, which was used in *Naked Gun 2 1/2: The Smell of Fear,* appears again in the film during a scene filmed in the business office of actress Louise Fletcher's character.

BASEketball (1998)

Crockett-like coonskin caps appear several times in this movie: cheerleaders for the San Antonio Defenders wear them, children's dolls wear them and one of the child actors wears one.

* An exclusive for *The Davy Crockett Almanac & Book of Lists.*

FRANK THOMPSON'S "DAVY AWARDS"*

Frank Thompson is a writer and film historian. His books include *Alamo Movies, Texas' First Picture Show, William A. Wellman, AMC's Great Christmas Movies, Abraham Lincoln: Twentieth Century Popular Portrayals*, and *Robert Wise: A Bio-Bibliography*. He has written several scripts and hundreds of articles, interviews, and reviews.

As far as we know, Davy Crockett made his first screen appearance in a movie in 1909. The film was called *Davy Crockett— In Hearts United*. The one-reeler starred Charles K. French but didn't make much of a splash; in fact, no prints are even known to have survived. But it served its purpose in getting the ex-Congressman, Alamo hero, half-horse, and half-alligator out of the pages of the almanacs and books, and onto the silver screen where he would thrive for the next century. And thrive he has. There have been at least twenty movie and television Davy's, played by now-forgotten actors like A. D. Sears (*Martyrs of the Alamo* in 1915) and miscast actors like Brian Keith (*The Alamo: 13 Days to Glory*, a 1987 TV movie). But there have also been indelible, immortal Davy's in the movies, like Fess Parker (*Davy Crockett, King of the Wild Frontier*) and John Wayne (*The Alamo*).

Here are the first (and I'm guessing the last) "Davy Awards."

BEST DAVY DEATH SCENE
John Wayne in *The Alamo*

Duke's Davy goes running toward the chapel, Robert Evans-style, torch in hand. A couple of Mexican soldiers move in for the kill but he demolishes them both with a stick or something. Then another soldier, a dismounted Cavalryman, pins Davy to the door like a buckskin-covered butterfly. You'd think that this would spell Crockett's finish, but no sir. With one mighty swing of his torch, Davy not only breaks off the lance that's currently sticking through him, but sends his attacker off to oblivion. That's one magic torch. But we aren't done yet. Davy staggers away, leaving a little gory graffiti on the door, forgets something, comes back to check, staggers away again, then flings the torch onto a pile of gunpowder barrels. Ka-blooey! It would have been quite devastating to the attacking Mexicans, if there were any in the remote vicinity.

WORST DAVY DEATH SCENE
Brian Keith in *The Alamo: 13 Days to Glory*

This is a revisionist Davy who doesn't swing "Old Betsy," doesn't fling a torch, and probably couldn't sing "Farewell to the Mountains" if you paid him. In the final clash, in which the Alamo defenders face defeat by bad editing, and dozens of Mexican soldiers, Davy does battle with a Bowie knife, swinging it wide in order to clear the brim of his enormous hat. When he's had enough of this, Davy thoughtfully helps a Mexican soldier by guiding a bayonet into his own chest. Even the doctor's scene from John Wayne's *The Alamo* is more dramatic and convincing.

MOST AMBIGUOUS DEATH SCENE
Fess Parker in *Davy Crockett, King of the Wild Frontier*

Ambiguous because he doesn't die. Yeah, now that's more like it!

MOST PATHETIC DAVY DEATH SCENE
Lane Chandler in *Heroes of the Alamo*

After the battle is over and Santa Anna is surveying the carnage with a satisfied sneer, something catches his eye. It's a wounded Crockett, crawling away. Santa Anna says, reasonably enough, "Kill that!" Immediately, one of his lackies smacks Davy on the head with a rifle butt. But oddly enough, where such a blow might render you or me a little whoozy in the extreme, it leads Crockett to say something like, "I'll be dang to ya!" (To be honest, I've never been able to really understand what he says.) But here's the point. After uttering these immortal words, he clutches his chest—yep, you read correctly—and dies. Which leads viewers to say, "Huh?"

BEST INTRODUCTION TO DAVY
Lane Chandler in *Heroes of the Alamo*

When Davy pulls up at the Alamo he isn't quite sure what he's doing there—and he doesn't care. "Let's see," he says, "It's Mexicans you're fightin', ain't it? Oh well, it doesn't matter. One fight's just like another to me and old Betsy here; I reckon I'll stay and help." And that's really about the last we see of him until, you know, "Kill that!"

BEST DAVY GRINS
Fess Parker in *Davy Crockett, King of the Wild Frontier*
Cullen Landis in *With Davy Crockett at the Fall of the Alamo*

It's a tie. Fess Parker's Davy tries twice—ineffectually both times—to grin down an opponent. First, he bares his old ivories to a bear in a bush, but to no avail. Later, he thinks his choppers will give him a little leverage against that rough-and-tumble Indian chief, Red Stick. He's mistaken. After that, he doesn't try again, even at the Alamo, where a grin or two would have been highly appreciated. But Cullen Landis indeed brings his grin with him to the Alamo. During the final battle, Landis' Davy has found a quiet corner to rip his shirt off and duke it out with a couple of Mexican soldiers who have conveniently lost their rifles and bayonets. He's doing pretty well, too, until he's finally outnumbered and ventilated. After cutting him like a carp, the attackers step away and Davy musters one last defiant grin—a little late in the game, if you ask me—and dies.

BEST SINGING DAVY
Fess Parker in *Davy Crockett, King of the Wild Frontier*

Well, there's really only one: Fess Parker. Is there a dry eye in your house when he croons "Farewell to the Mountains" just moments before leaving to sing with the Choir Invisible?

DAVY MOST LIKELY TO BE ON A SURFBOARD
John Schneider in *James A. Michener's "Texas"*

With his shoulder-length blonde hair and fringe-covered clothes, this Davy is more Haight-Ashbury than pure Tennessee.

STRONGEST DAVY
John Wayne in *The Alamo*

We have already discussed the damage Duke's Davy could do with a simple torch, but let's also remember earlier in the battle when he upends a horse, sending the rider flying ("Get off your high horse, mister!")

WORST DAVY HAT
Brian Keith in *The Alamo: 13 Days to Glory*
   'Nuff said.

BEST DAVY SIDEKICKS
Lige and Pinky in *With Davy Crockett at the Fall of the Alamo*
   Conventional wisdom would go for Georgie Russel or the Parson or Thimblerig. Personally, I lean toward the two sidekicks in the 1926 production *With Davy Crockett at the Fall of the Alamo*. One is Lige, "champion spitter of the South." He is a crusty old coot—crusty with tobacco juice, actually—and his last living act on this earth is spitting at a Mexican soldier's shako and smiling with satisfaction when it hits its mark. Davy's other pal in the movie is Pinky, one of the Alamo couriers who returned with bad news. During the last battle, Pinky is under the mistaken impression that he might better serve by running about with a large flag than by, say, killing enemy soldiers. Naturally, this course of actions leads, like paths of glory, but to the grave. When he's wounded and ready to give up, Pinky inspires what might be my favorite line in any Crockett movie. . . .

BEST DAVY LINE
Pinky in *With Davy Crockett at the Fall of the Alamo*
   "Up. Pinky, Up!" from *With Davy Crockett at the Fall of the Alamo*. Of course, there are other memorable Davy Lines: Arthur Hunnicutt's "They'll eat snakes before they get in here" from *The Last Command,* and John Wayne's "I never found the time," his gruff response to the Parson's "You never pray, do you Davy?" in *The Alamo*. And in *Alamo . . . The Price of Freedom,* Merrill Connally's Davy draws a bead on a Mexican soldier trotting across a drawbridge. Though someone suggests that the man is out of range, Davy fires and hits him. Smiling wryly he says, "That's what he was countin' on." Good line. But, of course, it's no "Up. Pinky, Up!"

BEST DAVY SPEECH
Arthur Hunnicutt in *The Last Command*
   Of course, John Wayne's "Republic" speech is right up there from *The Alamo*. And there's the speech in which Fess Parker ver-

bally flips off Congress in *Davy Crockett, King of the Wild Frontier*. It's a good speech in general, but especially notable in that it's the only time in any movie when Crockett ever describes himself as "half-horse, half-alligator." But the best of all Davy speeches is Arthur Hunnicutt's welcoming speech which he is "persuaded" to give soon after arriving in San Antonio. It sounds more like the legendary Crockett of the almanacs and the historical speechifier than any other single dialogue in any other Davy movie.

* An exclusive for *The Davy Crockett Almanac & Book of Lists*.

TOP 10 CROCKETT FOOD & DRINK ITEMS

Davy Crockett was an accomplished hunter who enjoyed fresh game. In his 1834 autobiography, *A Narrative of the Life of David Crockett of the State of Tennessee,* the famous frontiersman noted a number of animals that he successfully hunted, including bears, hawks, squirrels, and turkeys.

Crockett and food always seemed to go together, so it came as no surprise that the Davy Crockett Craze of the 1950s inspired many food and beverage producers to generate everything from cookies and lollipops, to cranberries and oysters. And the famous frontiersman's image graced the packages of additional items in the decades that followed; as a matter of fact, a number of present-day manufacturers still put Crockett's name on their products.

Here's a list of some of the more interesting food and drink items offered by producers over the years:

1. "Davy Crockett Blinded Tennessee Hydrated Bear Grease"
It doesn't sound like something tasty, but this product is

actually U.S. grade "A" honey produced by Florida's Tropical Blossom Honey Company in the 1980s. The eighteen-ounce bottle features a colorful comedic label depicting a tipsy Crockett with a powderhorn dripping honey.

2. "Crockett's Chocolate Raspberry"
A gourmet coffee produced in the 1990s by Texas' Ciafrani Coffee Company. The flavor is part of the company's "Texas Hero" line of coffees.

3. "Davy Crockett Ice Cream"
Made in pint, quart, and half-gallon sizes by Canada's Mount Royal Dairies Company in the 1950s. The label instructed kids to "save the lids" and "exchange them for official Davy Crockett merchandise."

4. "Little Davy Crockett Imitation Grape"
A 1950s liquid pick-me-up for young pioneers wearing plastic-fringed clothing.

5. "Davy Crockett Picture Card Bubble Gum"
Classic pink-colored bubble gum which accompanied the *Davy Crockett, King of the Wild Frontier* bubble gum cards issued by Topps during the summer of 1956.

6. "Davy Crockett Oysters"
Decades ago, the Crockett Seafood Company of Irvington, Virginia, sold these underwater delights in one gallon-sized tins with green and white lettering.

7. "Davy Crockett Candy"
During the 1950s, the Boston-based American Nut and Chocolate Company produced these confections in a small cardboard box, in which a small plastic toy was included—sort of a backwoods version of Cracker Jack.

8. "Crockett's Roasted Garlic Salsa"
This tasty offering is currently produced by the Fess Parker Winery & Vineyard. Now Fess is known as the "King of the Wine Frontier."

9. "Davy's Wrangler Seasonin'"
Another Fess Parker Winery & Vineyard product. The jar's label states: "Use on your favorite grub."

10. "Official Davy Crockett Candies and Toy"
The box weighed just 3/8 of an ounce, but the Super Novelty Candy Co. of Newark, New Jersey, packed it with "sugar, corn syrup, vegetable shortening, cocoa, salt, natural and artificial flavors, and U.S. certified colors."

THE DAVY CROCKETT DRIVE-IN*

The Davy Crockett Drive-In, located in Trenton-by-the-Sea, Maine, kept the spirit of the "King of the Wild Frontier" alive years after the mid-1950s Davy Crockett Craze had peaked.

Here are some tasty selections from a 1958 menu (with original prices). But just what was in the unidentified "Western Sandwich?"

SPECIALS
"Davy Crockett Special"
chicken salad roll, cole slaw, french fries $1.00

SANDWICHES
"Stockade" — grilled hamburger, garnish   .30
"Prairie Hen Special" — egg salad, garnish   .25
"Border County" — cheeseburger, garnish   .35
"Redskin Special" — frankfurter, garnish   .20
"Pioneer" — lettuce, tomato, and bacon, garnish   .35
"Warpath" — chopped ham and pickle   .35
"Western Sandwich"   .20
"Wilderness" — peanut butter   .20
"Fighting Spirit" — lobster roll, garnish   .75
"Lone Scout" — clam roll, garnish   .65

"Indian Creek" — crabmeat roll, garnish   .65
"Indian Raid" — cream chese and olive   .25
"Squirrel Gun Special" — chicken salad   .45
"Davy's Congressional Special" — grilled cheese   .35
"Range Rider Special" — grilled cheese and ham   .45
"General Andy" — ham sandwich   .35
"Davy's Garden Patch Special" —
    tomato and lettuce   .25

SUNDAES
"Davy Crockett Mountain Top"
    cocoanut ice cream, chocoloate sauce   .25
"Davy Crockett Birthday Special"
    peppermint ice cream, chocolate sauce   .25
"Davy Crockett Paleface"
    butterscotch sundae   .25
"Davy Crockett Open Range"
    walnut sundae   .25

* An exclusive for *The Davy Crockett Almanac & Book of Lists*.

DAVY CROCKETT—AN IDYL OF THE BACKWOODS

One of the most popular, long-running plays in American history featuring the same lead actor, *Davy Crockett—An Idyl of the Backwoods,* ran from from 1872 to 1896 and starred Frank Mayo in the title role. The play, also produced under the title *Davy Crockett; Or, Be Sure You're Right, Then Go Head,* was written by Frank Murdock and Frank Mayo. The historical Crockett had died twenty-six years before the play debuted. Frank Mayo entertained audiences in the show until 1896, when he died.

Here's a cast list from one of the play's undated productions:

ACT. 1	"Saddle Mending"
ACT. 2	"Wolves at the Door"
ACT. 3	"A Living Barrier"
ACT. 4	"Lochinvar's Ride"
ACT. 5	"Quickest Marriage on Record"

Davy Crockett	Mr. Frank Mayo
Major Roylston	Mr. W. B. Arnold
Neil Crampton	Mr. Edwin Frank
Oscar Crampton	Mr. H. A. Weaver, Jr.
Big Dan	Mr. J. Holmes
Yonkers	Mr. Joseph Richards
Briggs	Mr. Edward Secor
Watson	Mr. Joseph Brooks
Quickwitch	Mr. T. H. Conly
Parson Ainsworth	Mr. Samuel R. Reed
Eleanor Vaughan	Miss Affie Weaver
Dame Crockett	Mrs. J. L. Sanford
Bob Crockett	Clara Thropp
Little Sal	Baby Thropp

DAVY CROCKETT; OR; BE SURE YOU'RE RIGHT, THEN GO AHEAD

The popular play starring Frank Mayo was commemorated for its one-thousandth production at Corinthian Hall in Rochester, New York, on May 10, 1877. A special engraved silver program of the play was presented to Mayo by his fellow cast members. The program also stated that *Davy Crockett; Or; be Sure You're Right, Then Go Ahead* was first performed in the upper New York state city on September 23, 1872.

Notice that the cast billing is slightly different from the *Davy Crockett—An Idyl of the Backwoods* production. In addition, some character titles have been changed, and one, "Little Sal," has been omitted.

Davy Crockett	Mr. Frank Mayo
Major Roylston	J. C. Dunn
Oscar Crampton	W. B. Laurens
Neil Crampton	W. M. Dell
Mr. Ainsworth	John Weaver
Big Dan	H. Bingham
Yonkers	Geo. Gaston
Briggs	T. Conly
Watson	R. Thayer
Quickwitch	A. Wadsworth
Bob Crockett	David Rivers
Eleanor Vaughan	Josephine Laurens
Dame Crockett	Annie Douglas

DAVY CROCKETT COMIC BOOKS

Davy Crockett has appeared in scores of comic books. He's easily identifiable on the cover of many of them, like Dell Comics' *Davy Crockett at the Alamo* in 1955, but he's sometimes found within the pages of other titles, like Quality Comics' *Marmaduke Mouse* in 1956.

Here's a list of Crockett comics, from the familiar to the obscure:

Davy Crockett, Indian Fighter	(1955, Dell Comics #631)
Davy Crockett at the Alamo	(1955, Dell Comics #639)
Davy Crockett, King of the Wild Frontier	(1955, Dell Giant)
Davy Crockett in the Keelboat Race	(1955, Dell Comics #664)
Davy Crockett and the River Pirates	(1955, Dell Comics #671)
Davy Crockett, King of the Wild Frontier	(1963, Gold Key reprint #1)
Davy Crockett, King of the Wild Frontier	(1969, Gold Key reprint #2)

Walt Disney's "Davy Crockett in the Raid at Piney Creek"	(1955, Hudson Motors free distribution booklet)
Mickey Mouse in Frontierland	(1956, Dell Comics #1)
Donald Duck Beach Party	(1956, Dell Comics #3)
Donald Duck Beach Party	(1957, Dell Comics #4)
Donald Duck Beach Party	(1958, Dell Comics #5)
It's Game Time	(1955, DC Comics #1)
Tomahawk	(1955-1956, DC Comics #35 & #36)
Frontier Fighters	(1955-1956, DC Comics #1-8)
All-Star Western	(1971, DC Comics reprint #8)
Davy Crockett, Frontier Fighter	(1955-1957, Charlton Comics #1-8)
Wild Hunter	(1955-1957, Charlton Comics #1-6)
Hunting With Davy Crockett	(n.d., Charlton Comics free distribution)
Heroes of the Wild Frontier	(1956, Ace Comics #27) (this is actually Ace Comics #1)
Frontier Fighter Davy Crockett	(1951, Avon Comics)
Fighting Davy Crockett	(1955, Avon Comics)
Davy Crockett	(1955, Classics Illustrated #129)
Young Davy Crockett	(1955, "Another Captain Fortune Fable," Vital Publications free distribution)
Davy Crockett Meets Sam Houston	(1955, "From The Diary of Captain Fortune," Vital Publications free distribution)
Davy Crockett at the Alamo	(1955, "Captain Fortune Presents," Vital Publications free distribution)
Davy Crockett Visits Federation's Frontier	(8-page Federation of Jewish Philanthropies fundraiser publication; n.d.)
Forbidden Worlds	(1955, American Comic Group #39)

Davy Crockett Western Tales	(1956, Harvey Comics, #31 & #32)
World Famous Heroes	(1941, Comic Corporation #1)
Indian Fighter	(1951, Youthful Magazine #6)
Tex Granger	(1949, Commended Comics #20)
Marmaduke Mouse	(1956, Quality Comics #58)
Two-Fisted Tales	(1952, EC Comics #28)
Sgt. Rock	(1979, DC Comics #324)
Stupid	(1993, Image Comics #1. Crockett appears once without identification.)
Beethoven	(1994, Harvey Comics #1. Crockett appears once without identification.)

HOWARD BENDER'S TOP 10 FAVORITE DAVY CROCKETT COMIC BOOKS*

Howard Bender is a professional illustrator, Davy Crockett collector, and creator of Crocktcraze@aol.com, the Internet's number one site dedicated to the legend of Davy Crockett. He has created art for *The Alamo Journal* and has appeared on the television show *Collectors F/X*. Bender specializes in collecting Davy Crockett comics and newspaper comic art.

Here's the list of his favorite Davy Crockett comic books:

1. *Forbidden Worlds*, #39 (1955)

American Comic Group's *Fordbidden Worlds* #39 gave us "The Davy Crockett Mystery!" written by editor Richard E. Hughes and illustrated by my good friend, Kurt Schaffenberger. Talk about your oddball stories. This one has our frontier hero, almost dead from the Battle of the Alamo, drinking from a fountain of youth that allows him to live on and fight in every major American war up to World War II, where, dying heroically, he decomposes into a clump of smoldering bones.

2. Walt Disney's "Davy Crockett in the Raid at Piney Creek" (1955)

This was a small, free distribution booklet produced by Hudson, an American Motors automobile. However, this litte item has it all. Fess Parker's color photo covers the front and back with top-notch art by artist Jesse Marsh, who is best known for his work in Dell Comics' *Tarzan* series. The back cover features Fess Parker in full Crockett get-up, standing behind a 1955 Hudson Hornet. This giveaway is a Crockett must—and worth every penny.

3. *Davy Crockett Western Tales, #32* (1956)

Harvey Comics' Davy Crockett Western Tales #31 and #32 were Joe (*Captain America*) Simon and Jack (*Fantastic Four*) Kirby's response to the Davy Crockett Craze. Joe recalls: "That was the craze going around; Davy Crockett was a big hit on TV. According to the publishers, these trends were very important in the comic book industry. So, we, Jack and I, were ready and available to leap into the fray, as they say, to do a quick book. And that's what happened. We also did Jim Bowie in issue #33." *Davy Crockett Western Tales, #32* features Davy and a boy sidekick, Daniel, locking horns with "King Ram" and learning a lesson in fair play. This is Simon and Kirby at their very best in western lore.

4. *Davy Crockett, King of the Wild Frontier* (1955)

A Dell Comic "Giant" with one hundred pages of Davy Crockett comics and stories, featuring art by Jesse Marsh packaged between two glossy, full-color Fess Parker cover photos. This book not only has our frontier hero going to Congress and the Alamo, but includes a "Dictionary" showcasing some of Davy's more colorful words and phrases like "speechifier" and "riproariously."

5. *Tomahawk,* #35 (1955)

Frederick Ray drew the "Young Davy Crockett" appearances for DC Comics' Tomahawk #35 and #36. This one has young Davy winning the prized "White Buffalo" in a shooting contest.

6. *The Story of the Alamo* (1955)

Frererick Ray, who drew *Superman, Batman,* and *Tomahawk* for DC Comics, wrote and drew this valuable Alamo reference comic book/magazine, which is still on sale (in reprint) at the Alamo in San Antonio, Texas.

7. *Davy Crockett and the River Pirates* (1955)

This Dell Comics four-color publication (#671) features a great purple and green cover. Inside, Davy, George Russel, and Mike Fink fight the river pirates, thanks to Jesse Marsh's artwork. This comic, along with *Davy Crockett in the Great Keelboat Race* (#664), are the most difficult to find of the five newsstand Davy Crockett Dell comic books.

8. *Mickey Mouse in Frontierland* (1956)

Just when you thought you couldn't shoehorn another Davy Crockett comic book onto the newsstands in the 1950s, Disney came out with a younger, cuter version for its animated cartoon titles. *Mickey Mouse in Frontierland,* #1, published by Dell Comics, features Li'l Davy Crockett running around with Little Hiawatha, grinning down "b'ars" and singing "The Ballad of Davy Crockett." All this with Mickey, Donald, and crew in buckskins and coonskin caps.

9. *Two-Fisted Tales,* #28 (1952)

This EC Comics issue has a six-page "Alamo" story written by editor-writer Harvey Kurtzman (who helped give us *Mad* magazine), and artist John Severn. The story shows the horrors of war through the sympathetic eyes of a Mexican soldier who has been ordered to execute the last surving Alamo defenders. This is alas, one of the first stories that John Severn ever inked over his own pensil art. Note: Though John believes that Crockett surrendered at the Alamo, he depicted Davy "giving 'em what 'fer" as he fought to the end with a cutlass in one hand and a flintlock in the other.

10. *Davy Crockett, Frontier Fighter, #5* (1956)
     This is my favorite Charlton Comics cover. It showcases our buckskin hero, movie poster-style, in front of a horde of Indians. The issue also features my favorite Davy Crockett story, "The Tale Spinner," which has Davy riding a bolt of lightning clear around the world. It's electrifyin.'

     * An exclusive for *The Davy Crockett Almanac & Book of Lists*

HOWARD BENDER'S FIVE RAREST DAVY CROCKETT COMIC BOOKS*

Davy Crockett, Frontier Fighter #7	(Charlton Comics, 1957)
Davy Crockett, Frontier Fighter #8	(Charlton Comics, 1957)
Hunting With Davy Crockett	(Charlton Comics free distribution, 1956)
Forbidden Worlds #39	(American Comic Group, 1955)
Davy Crockett Christmas Book	(Vital Publications free distribution, 1955)

     * An exclusive for *The Davy Crockett Almanac & Book of Lists*

MURRAY WEISSMANN'S TOP TEN DISNEY DAVY CROCKETT COLLECTIBLES*

     Murray Weissmann has probably the world's largest collection of Davy Crockett/Alamo memorabilia. Among the thousands of items in his collection are hundreds of items licensed under the authority of Walt Disney Productions. Notes Weissmann: "Although the items produced or licensed by the Walt Disney Company accounted for only about 10% of these collectibles, they are generally considered to be of the best quality and are among some of the rarest items." This list is more accurately titled "Murray Weissmann's Ten Favorite, rarest, and most interesting Walt Disney Official Davy Crockett Collectibles."

1. 24-Sheet Billboard-sized Poster

This was produced to promote the 1955 theatrical release of *Davy Crockett, King of the Wild Frontier.* A very rare item, the poster is far too large for display in a home and remains folded in sections, never having been mounted.

2. Original Artwork for the *Legends of Davy Crockett*

This original artwork measures 20" x 14" and is a watercolor painting on cardboard for the book published by the Whitman Publishing Company in 1955. The painting was reproduced for the book's front cover, spine, and back cover. One of a kind item.

3. Accordian

This toy instrument measures 9" x 7" x 5" when closed. Aside from its rarity, it is interesting because it reproduces twelve scenes from the 1954-1955 TV episodes as color drawings which are not seen on any other toy.

4. Quart Ice Cream Container

This cardboard container is extremely rare and was originally produced by the Mount Royal Dairies & Company Ltd. of Montreal. It stands 5 1/2" high with a 4 1/4" diameter. The container originally contained vanilla ice cream, and was produced as a tie-in product for the theatrical release of *Davy Crockett, King of the Wild Frontier* in Canada. The container displays three black & white photos of Fess Parker and an ad which states: "Free! Kids, save the lids of pints, quarts and half-gallon cartons, exchange them for Official Crockett merchandise." One side of the carton is printed in English, the other in French. The ice cream has long since been consumed.

5. Disneyland China Plate

The ten-inch, cream-colored china plate has a silver border, and shows Fess Parker with a background of the Alamo battle and Crockett in Congress. The plate is titled "Walt Disney's Davy Crockett, King of the Wild Frontier." The words "Disneyland" and "Frontierland" also appear prominently on the front of the plate. The reverse states: "Copyright Walt Disney Productions, manufactured by Eleanore Welborn Art productions, Monterey, California." The plate was originally sold in Frontierland in Disneyland. It is extremely rare and is coveted by both Crockett and Disneyland collectors.

6. Bubble Gum Card Boxes

Although the two sets of Davy Crockett bubble gum cards (orange backs and green backs) produced by Topps Chewing Gum, Inc. of Brooklyn, New York, are relatively easy to find, unopened packs of these cards are much more unusual to find. And the boxes that these packs were sold from are very unusual, most having been discarded after the packs were sold. Both sets of cards came in one-cent and five-cent packs and each came in a different box. The one-cent box held 120 packs and the five-cent box held 24 packs. Graphics on the boxes were similar: The one-cent box features Crockett and Red Stick, the Creek chief; the five-cent box depicts Crockett at the Alamo.

7. Super 8mm Film

Probably the only film produced for consumers, this super 8mm color film with magnetic sound was made in France for distribution in Canada. Titled *Davy Crockett et Le Chef Indien* ("Davy Crockett and the Indian Chief"), it consists of 8mm film on a five-inch plastic reel in a box with a color photo of Davy Crockett. The film depicts Davy's hand-to-hand fight with Red Stick at the conclusion of the "Davy Crockett, Indian Fighter" edpisode. Very unusual.

8. Suede Advertising Signs

Two of these are known to exist, both cut with irregular borders to resemble animal hides. The larger one measures 51" x 42" with a color portrait of Fess Parker as Crockett. The smaller sign measures 32" x 21" and features crossed rifles, a powder horn, and a tomahawk. Above this is written "Davy Crockett Marshall of Walt Disney's Frontierland." On back of both items is the statement: "For use only with the display and promotion of Davy Crockett (Fess Parker) Official Walt Disney designs and products produced only by manufacturers authorized and licensed by Walt Disney Productions."

9. Original Comic Book Galley Sheet

This galley sheet in black ink was designed for the *Davy Crockett at the Alamo* comic book. The sheet measures 23½" x 16½" and depicts the artwork for page seven of Dell comic book #639 before the colors were added. It is labeled DCOS #639, p. 7.

10. Giant Cut-Out Standee

I am ending this list with an item so unusual that it is not part of my collection. As a matter of fact, I have never seen this item. It is a "Full Color Giant 7-Foot Cut-Out Standee" of Fess Parker as Davy Crockett. It is advertised in the pressbook for the theatrical feature film *Davy Crockett, King of the Wild Frontier,* and was designed to stand outside the theater where the film was shown.

* An exclusive for *The Davy Crockett Almanac & Book of Lists*

PAUL DEVITO'S TOP 10 NON-DISNEY DAVY CROCKETT COLLECTIBLES*

Known as a "Super Collector" by the television program *Collectors F/X,* Paul DeVito has assembled one of the largest collections of Davy Crockett memorabilia. Walt Disney licensed several hundred items under the title "Davy Crockett, King of the

Wild Frontier," but since the famous nineteenth century back-woodsman's name was not protected by copyright, thousands of manufacturers in the 1950s cranked out just about everything they could imagine with a Crockett image or name on it. It's been over forty years since the Davy Crockett Craze and Paul DeVito has nearly all of the original merchandise items. However, when it comes to rarity, Paul DeVito notes the following:

1. Bicycle

This two-wheeler was manufactured by the J. C. Higgins Company. The cream-colored bike has Davy Crockett's name and image in brown graphics on the chain guard.

2. Pocket Watch

This timepiece was made by the Davy Crockett Watch Company. Both the watch and its box feature graphics of the Alamo and Davy Crockett.

3. Bedroom Set

This furniture set consists of a bed and two bureaus. Each item features rifle graphics and a carved picture of the famous frontiersman. As an added embellishment, carved powder horns serve as the bureau handles.

4. Arcade Rifle Shoot Game

This is a full arcade target game that stands about five-feet tall. Multicolored Davy Crockett logos are featured on the glass. The animal targets pop up and rotate.

5. Shoeshine Box

This wooden box is decorated with Crockett decals. Like all shoeshine boxes, it has a place to put a shoe.

6. Diaper Bag

This item was made by the Brockton Manufacturing Company. The diaper bag comes complete with two diapers, two safety pins, a bottle, and a clothesline.

7. Pipe Display

This sixteen-inch high display features a dozen, four-inch long pipes with round red-and-white Crockett tags. The pipes are made in two color combinations: solid brown and brown & white. The orange, black & white display card also exhibits a large picture of Davy.

8. Bar-B-Que Grill

This backyard cooking item was made by the RMP Corporation. It was nothing more than a generic metal charcoal grill of the period. However, the box showed Davy Crockett cooking while children looked on.

9. Revolving Scene Clock in Box

This timepiece has a large metal figure of Crockett with a clear plastic section that depicts the frontier hero looking at Indians and wagons.

10. Fishing Set on Card

This item was made by the N. Y. Toy and Game Company. The bright red card, which features a picture of Davy Crockett, comes with everything you need to land the big one.

* An exclusive for *The Davy Crockett Almanac & Book of Lists*

DAVY CROCKETT AND "THE SIMPSONS"

No one can ever accuse Davy Crockett of not having a sense of humor. His autobiography, *A Narrative of the Life of David Crockett of the State of Tennessee,* is filled with entertaining backwoods language and a genuine sense of fun. To be sure, the Davy Crockett almanacs printed from 1835 to 1856 are an even richer source of humor. The almanacs are replete with outrageous tall tales and exaggerated verbiage. It's no wonder that the equally outlandish animated television series, *The Simpsons,* has made references to Davy Crockett on more than one occasion. First of all, the Simpson family resides in Springfield, which was founded by a coonskin cap-wearing frontiersman by the name of Jebediah Obediah Zacariah Jedediah Springfield. The town's founder followed somewhat in Davy Crockett's footsteps by claiming to kill a bear with his bare hands, but in an episode titled "The Telltale Head," modern historians suggest that the bear actually killed Springfield with his bare claws.

Episode Title: "Treehouse of Horror II"

In this Frankenstein-inspired episode, which first aired on January 31, 1991, Springfield nuclear power plant entrepreneur C. Montgomery Burns celebrates the creation of his ten-foot high Homer Simpson-like robot, by dancing around with Homer's brain on his head and shouting, "Look at me, I'm Davy Crockett!"

Episode Title: "The Otto Show"

This episode, which first aired on April 23, 1992, features Bart Simpson attempting to become a heavy metal guitarist after attending his first rock concert. During the concert, Bart's aunt, Selma Bouvier, sees Bart's father, Homer, who is wearing an old fringed jacket, and exclaims: "There goes Davy Crockett and his baldskin cap."

DAVY CROCKETT'S TITLES IN
"THE BALLAD OF DAVY CROCKETT"

Tom Blackburn and George Bruns' popular 1954 song contained many descriptive titles of Davy Crockett besides the familiar "King of the Wild Frontier."

Here's a list of all of his lyrical titles from the twenty-verse song plus another (*) that was performed in the three-part TV trilogy's sound track, but was not included in the original sheet music.

"King of the Wild Frontier"
"The Buckskin Pioneer" *
"The Man Who Don't Know Fear"
"The Bucksin Buccaneer"
"The Champion of us All"
"Choice of the Whole Frontier"
"The Canebrake Congressman"

DAVY CROCKETT SHOWS UP IN THE STRANGEST PLACES

Davy Crockett's image, legend, ballad, coonskin cap, and other mass marketed merchandise pop up in the strangest of places—in addition to the movies made by David Zucker.

Here are a few moments that you may not have noticed:

Movie Moments
The Lemon Sisters
This 1989 comedy, starring Diane Keaton, Carol Kane, and Kathyryn Grody, was filmed in Atlantic City, New Jersey. In one scene, some of the characters' possessions are stacked outside a boardwalk casino-hotel. In the pile of items are a bucksin jacket, a muzzleloading rifle, and a Walt Disney *Davy Crockett, King of the Wild Frontier* bookbag.

Back to the Future
Michael J. Fox travels back in time in this 1985 comedy. In one scene, he enters a store on "November 5, 1955" and hears "The Ballad of Davy Crockett" sung by Fess Parker, playing from a jukebox.

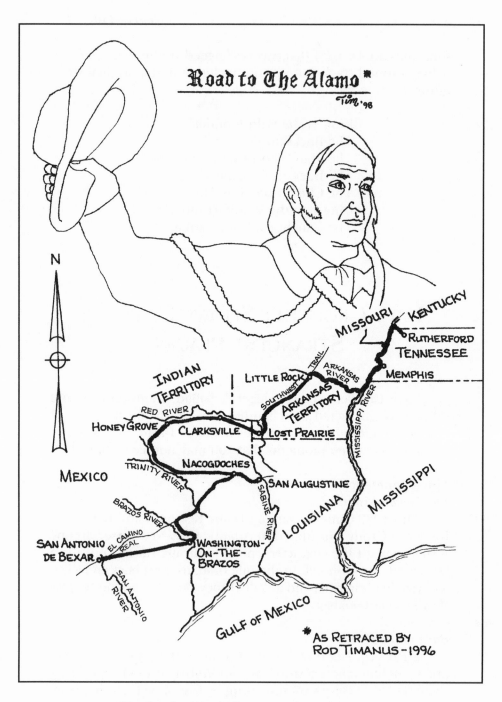

"Road to the Alamo" illustrations by Rod Timanus.

People Who Wore Davy Crockett Coonskin Caps
A Christmas Story

This wonderfully wacky 1983 Christmas tale about an American family in the 1940s features a neighborhood bully named "Scut Farcus" (played by actor Zach Ward) who wears a coonskin cap.

"Ralph Kramden"

Jackie Gleason's enduring character from TV's *The Honeymooners* occasionally wore his coonskin cap as a member of the Racoon Lodge.

The Fat Boys

Members of this rap group frequently wore their coonskin caps while creating funky, hip-hop sounds in the 1980s.

Dutchess of York

Sarah Ferguson wore her coonskin cap while touring Canada in 1987. One British newspaper retitled her "Fergie Crockett, Queen of the Wild Frontier."

"CROCKETT BY FIRELIGHT"*

This original poem, written by Dr. Floyd Collins of the english department at Quincy University, Quincy, Illinois, depicts the famous frontiersman at the Alamo. Crockett is waiting by a fire in front of the Alamo church prior to the imminent predawn assault on March 6, 1836.

> To thwart the evening chill, John Crockett
> Would daw a deep tankard of his own stock
> From a three-staved cask. A leather-aproned
> Tavern host grown stout with the memory
> Of wielding the flintlock pegged above the bar

At the battle of King's Mountain, he often
Took the measure of his stripling son
With a birch rod. Young David never chafed

At spliting fence rails with maulk and wedge,
But when his father sent him to scratch
A slate at the age of twelve, he bolted.
Now he hunkers by firelight in the chalk-white
Glow of the limestone chapel, his name
A legend in columns back East. An iron horse
Hitched to a congregation of vapors,
The *Davy Crockett* beats its way

From Saratoga to Schenectady
Belched a cloud of sparks. Crockett closes
His eyes a moment, rides the cool
Slipstream of twenty-five miles an hour
Beneath the stars of the old republic.
Yet he prefers the tall chestnut mare
With the blaze on her forehead. She bore
His raw-boned bulk from Gibson County.

To San Antonio, helped him escape
The industrial reek of the seaboard states,
Whig intrigue, the glib political
Machine of Jackson's Kitchen Cabinet,
Inexorable gears that notch and wheel,
Grinding the common man to bonemeal.
Stump oratory came easy at first,
Each ballot like a glimmering perch
Snatched from a millrace with the hook
Of native wit. But Crockett's constituency
Went straight to hell at the August polls.
Before the ripe persimmons fumed
On a killing frost and the black bear gorged,
He struck out for Texas, the bluestream prairies
Rolling way under the hooves of buffalo.
He forsook "Pretty Betsey," the engraved

Pennsylvania rifle inlaid with gold
And german silver, a weapon shaped
By the Gods and Covetousness. He chose
Instead his percussion muzzle-loader,
Its copper nipple, and the smoke-smudged
Sights that gleam no warning. Tonight
He fed his fire in the Alamo courtyard
A shoot of resinous cedar; an ember popped,

Leapt the flames, and lit like a flea on the toe
Of his boot: "Lice and such varmits as these
Always quit a dying man," he observed,
"I'm good for a few years yet." Others roared,
But he swallowed like it was hard medicine,
A seraphic ghoul resplendent in frock coat
And bullion tassels, Santa Anna offered
A battalion of *fusileros* for slaughter

Nine days ago. How many yeoman-crowned
Bullhide shakos did Crockett topple
Between the mud-chinked *jacales* south
Of the mission outworks? Before the sun
Turns the evening mist to a blood-red dawn.
He foresees a full-scale assault. A torch
Spindles and wisps near the low barracks wall.
Women and children dream on burnished straw.

* An exclusive for *The Davy Crockett Almanac & Book of Lists*

CROCKETT POSSESSIONS AT THE ALAMO*

David Crockett died at the Alamo on March 6, 1836. Although nothing that Crockett wore or carried with him at the Alamo has survived, a number of his possessions have been donated to the famous mission-fortress over the years by individuals. These objects are either on display inside the Alamo church or carefully stored away in the temperature controlled archives of the Alamo Curator's office.

Here's a list of Crockett's possessions at the Alamo in San Antonio, Texas:

- two rifles
- two shot pouches
- shot flask
- bullet mold
- hunting bag
- powder can
- straight razor
- letter of transfer document signed by Crockett
- locket with a lock of Crockett's hair
- bear hunting knife
- law book
- buckskin vest
- tin box and beard brush
- leather wallet

PLUS
- Crockett Family fork
- wooden ladder back chair made by Crockett
- chimney stone, log, and wooden peg from Crockett's cabin
- cedar slab from Crockett's well
- quilt made by Elizabeth Patton Crockett, David's second wife
- boy's shirt from the Crockett Family

* An exclusive for *The Davy Crockett Almanac & Book of Lists*

PAST PRESIDENTS OF THE DIRECT DESCENDANTS OF DAVID CROCKETT*

The Direct Descendants of David Crockett is an international organization of Crockett's relatives and admirers. Founded in 1981 and organized in 1984, the Direct Descendants of David Crockett maintain three membership categories: "Direct Descendant" (members related directly through Crockett and his two wives: Polly and Elizabeth); "Cousin" (members related to Crockett through his brothers and sisters); and "Friend" (members who are not related to Crockett).

The Direct Descendants of David Crockett currently has several hundred members and holds large celebrations every other year, alternating between sites in Tennessee and Texas. In addition, the Direct Descendants of David Crockett publishes a periodic newsletter title *Go Ahead.*

Here's a list of the organization's past presidents:

1984-1986	Jim Dumas
1986-1988	Jim Dumas
1988-1990	Leonard Stasney
1990-1992	Joy Bland
1992-1994	Francis John
1994-1996	Joy Bland
1996-1998	Francis John
1998-2000	Charles Robertson

* An exclusive for *The Davy Crockett Almanac & Book of Lists*

CROCKETT IN THE SCHOOL BOOKS

David Crockett is mentioned in nearly every secondary American History text book. After all, he was a veteran of the

Creek Indian War, served three terms in the U.S. House of Representatives, and fought at the Alamo. However, the capsulized description of Crockett has varied from text to text. He is most frequently mentioned as one of the Alamo defenders. In some instances, he his described in chapters dealing with the American frontier. In the 1977 edition of *Rise of the American Nation,* nearly an entire page of text ("Davy Crockett's Advice on Politics") is devoted to the famous frontiersman via an excerpt from the 1836 book *Col. Crockett's Exploits and Adventures in Texas.*

Here's a sample list of textbooks—arranged chronologically—and what they've said about the "King of the Wild Frontier:"

People and Our Country (1982)

"Although uneducated and inexperienced, Crockett was a Whig, and Webster and Clay welcomed him with open arms. He toured New England at the Whig's expense and was helped by his memoirs, the *Autobiography of David Crockett.* . . . As a presidential candidate, though, Crockett never made it. He died in the Alamo in 1836 during the Texas Revolution."

The American Pageant: A History of the Republic (1983)

"The semi-literate Davy Crockett was elected to the legislature of Tennessee mainly on the basis of his prowess with the rifle."

Exploring United States History (1984)

"One such backwoods politician was the legendary pathfinder Davy Crockett. When the tall trapper first took a seat in the Tennessee legislature, he was called the 'gentleman from the cane,' because he hailed from the state's western canebrake country. He also quickly became known for his story tellling ability. That talent helped him win a place in Congress."

A Proud Nation (1989)

"Davy Crockett was 49 when he came to Texas from Tennessee. Crockett was a legendary frontiersman, and it was claimed that he could shoot off the wick of a candle at a distance of 100 yards. He was one of the last to die at the Alamo, and was later reported to have killed about two hundred Mexican soldiers by himself."

A People and a Nation: A History of the United States (1990)
"For urbanized people increasingly distant from the frontier, popular plays brought to life the mythical Wild West and Old South through stories of Davy Crockett, Buffalo Bill, and Civil War romances."

The American People: Creating a Nation and a Society (1994)
"David Crockett, one of Jackson's soldiers, later reported that the militia volunteers shot down the Red Sticks 'like dogs.'"

DESCRIPTIONS OF DAVID CROCKETT

What did David Crockett look like? That's a difficult question to answer with absolute certainty. Since he died a decade before daguerreotype images captured people's countenances for posterity, there is no "photographic" record of the famous frontier hero. And the several contemporary paintings of Crockett that survive are not uniform with regards to his appearance. However, there are a few nineteenth century descriptions of what David Crockett looked like.

Here are two independent descriptions of Crockett which are similar with regards to his height, weight, and complexion:

The Cincinnati Mirror and Western Gazette of Literature and Science February 21, 1835
"This was Colonel Crockett— . . . he was about six feet high—stoutly built—his hands and feet were particularly small for a man of his appearance and character . . . His complexion was swarthy; his cheek bones high; his nose large, and designed to favor an Indian's. His hair was long, dark and curly-looking, rather uncombed than carefully attended to."

John L. Jacobs November 22, 1884 (recollection)

"He was about six feet high, weighed about two hundred pounds, had no surplus flesh, broad shouldered, stood erect, was a man of great physical strength, of fine appearance, his cheeks mantled with a rosy hue, eyes vivacious, and in form, had no superior."

OTHER PUBLISHED DEATHS OF DAVY CROCKETT

Within weeks of the fall of the Alamo in 1836, reports of Crockett's death appeared in American newspapers. Some newspapers reported that the famous ex-Congressman died fighting; however, others suggested that he was captured and later executed. Ever since those first published reports, authors and writers have speculated about Crockett's final moments. Some authors used contemporary accounts which were previously published.

Here's a summary of those accounts from various books (not counting those previously cited in the "A" to "Z" section):

The Alamo: America's Thermoplylae" (n.d./late nineteenth century)

"The last two men killed were Travis and Colonel Crockett. . . ."

Alter, Robert Edmond: *Two Sieges of the Alamo* (1965)

"Sergeant Felix Nuñez (from whom we learn of the Tennessean who fought alone with his back to the corral wall) implies that this one American woodsman was indeed the might Crockett."

Archer, Olin W.: *The Alamo: 1836-1936* (1936)

"But before excited Mexicans could pick off the last of the

four, there was one more shot, the last cannon fired by the defenders. Crockett's body lay at the west gun station."

Austin, Mrs. Stephen F.: *The Alamo* (n.d./nineteenth century)
"As the remainder of the garrison stood back of him, reloading and handing him their weapons, Crockett guarded the main door to the chapel until he fell."

Barrett, Monte: *Tempered Blade* (1946)
"When his gun was finally engulfed Crockett went down defending it with his clubbed rifle."

Bennett, Leonora: *Historical Sketch and Guide to the Alamo* (1904)
"Crockett was among the last to die. His "Betsy' made many a Mexican rue the day he had found the army, and when there was no more time to load, he clubbed many a foe to death with his gun before he finally succumbed, his body bullet-ridden for minutes before he gave up the struggle."

Burke, James Wakefield: *The Blazing Dawn* (1975)
"David's arm is blown off, his companions killed instantly. Trailing blood and strings of pulverized flesh and bone, David steps into the clearing of the hallway. Yelling fiercely, he cries I'm still here! Come and get me!' A hail of gunfire cuts him down."

Chabot, Frederick Charles: *The Alamo: Altar of Texas Liberty* (1931)
"Crockett is reported to have been standing calmly, proudly with his clubbed rifle in hand dealing death to the foe with an unerring aim."

Chabot, Frederick Charles: *The Alamo: Mission, Fortress and Shrine* (1936)
"Crockett was shot down in a room in the low barrack, near the gate, where he had taken refuge. His body was found just inside the doorway to the Baptistry."

Chemerka, William R.: The Alamo Almanac & Book of Lists (1997)

"Crockett was killed during the March 6 assault. However, a modern debate continues about how Crockett died."

Chidsey, Donald Barr: *The Fall of the Alamo* **(1961)**

"Some of the Texans died right there, among them Davy Crockett, who, with no time to reload, had been laying about him with a smoking, clubbed Betsy when at last, the rush engulfed him."

Claiborne, Arie M.: *The Story of the Alamo* **(1901)**

"Crockett too fell early in the fight, but he left near him a little mound of the dead that he had slain."

DeShields, James T.: *Tall Men With Long Rifles* **(1935)**

"[Crockett] was killed in a room of the mission. A corporal ordered the passage cleared of those who were being pressed forward, a volley was fired almost point blank and the last defender of the Alamo fell forward—dead."

Ellis, Edward S.: *Remember the Alamo* **(1914)**

"Crockett made so sign, but General Castrillon, accepting his silence as submission, stopped the fighting and hurried the few steps to where Santa Anna, his swarthy face aflame with rage, stood watching the struggle. A volley closed the career of the last six of the Alamo garrison."

Fehrenbach, T. R.: *Lone Star: A History of Texas and Texans* **(1968)**

"Mexican accounts say, probably accurately, that a few defenders vainly attempted to surrender. These, who may have included Crockett, were shot."

Fisher, Leonard Everett: *The Alamo* **(1987)**

"Toward the west, and in the small fort opposite the city, we found the body of Colonel Crockett."

Ford, John Salmon: *Origin and Fall of the Alamo,*
March 6, 1836 (1896)
"Sergeant Becerra was of the opinion that the two last men killed were Travis and Colonel Crockett, though he admitted he did not know them personally and might be mistaken as to their identity."

Groneman, Bill: *Alamo Defenders* **(1990)**
"David Crockett died fighting during the Battle of the Alamo while defending his assigned area in front of the chapel."

Hirschfeld, Burt: *After The Alamo: The Story of the Mexican War* **(1960)**
"A Mexican lieutenant finally dealt him a crashing sword-blow above the right eye, and David Crockett went down."

Jakes, John: *The Furies* **(1976)**
"Colonel Crockett went down with ten, maybe twenty on top of him."

Karl, Dennis: *Glorious Defiance: Last Stands Throughout History* **(1990)**
"He sprang at him and dealt him a deadly blow with his sword, just above the right eye, which felled him to the ground, and in an instant he was pierced by no less than twenty bayonets."

Long, Jeff: *Duel of Eagles* **(1990)**
"The Go Ahead Man [Crockett] quit. He did more than quit. He lied. He dodged. He denied his role in the fighting."

Michener, James: *Texas* **(1985)**
"A Mexican officer claimed that the last of the famous defenders to survive was Davy Crockett. 'He hid under a pile of women's clothes and he begged and pleaded and wept when we trapped him. Said he would do anything if we spared him, but we shot him in contempt.' Unlikely, that."

Monroe Democrat April 5, 1836
"Davy Crocket [sic] not dead. The report of the eccentric Davy Crockett is not true. He started (says the letter) on a hunting expedition to the Rocky Mountains, and then dropped down into Texas; but we expect him home early in the Spring."

Murphy, Keith: *Battle of the Alamo* **(1979)**
"Near where Crockett fell, lay the bodies of seventeen dead Mexican soldiers."

Myers, John: *The Alamo* **(1948)**
"The Tennessean bashed, slashed, smashed, crushed, stamped, and rent apart the squads upons squads that came to them. Crockett and two of his men were reported to have been found in a heap with seventeen dead Mexicans."

Nofi, Albert: *The Alamo and the Texas War for Independence* **(1992)**
"It is probable that the story told by de la Péna (in which Crockett surrendered) is correct."

Petite, Mary Deborah: *1836 Facts About the Alamo and the Texas War for Independence* **(1999)**
"David Crockett died at the Alamo. This is all we know for sure."

Potter, R. M.: *The Fall of the Alamo* **(1860)**
"When he [Crockett] sallied down to meet his fate in the face of the foe, (he) was shot down."

Ray, Frederick: *The Story of the Alamo* **(1955)**
"Crockett and his Tennessean riflemen fell in the area fronting the chapel, surrounded by the bodies of the Mexicans they had slain . . ."

Rice, James: *Texas Jack at the Alamo* **(1989)**
"Davy Crockett killed eight Mexicans and wounded several more with his clubbed rifle before he was surrounded and killed."

Richards, Norman: *The Story of the Alamo* **(1970)**
"Then Davy Crockett fell dead, surrounded by enemy dead."

Santos, Richard G.: *Santa Anna's Campaign Against Texas, 1835-1836* **(1968)**
"David Crockett, a well-known naturalist from North America, was among the captured. Santa Anna severely reprimanded Castrillon for sparing their lives and ordered the Texans to be killed."

Shackford, James Atkins: *David Crockett: The Man and the Legend* **(1956)**
"David's death was quite undramatic, that he was one of the first to fall, and that he died unharmed,"

Shephard, Seth: *The Fall of the Alamo: An Oration* **(1889)**
"It was near this (artillery) platform after the battle, the body of Davy Crockett was pointed out to Santa Anna, surrounded by heaps of slain Mexicans, some of whom bore marks of his clubbed rifle."

Templeton, R. L.: *Alamo Soldier: The Story of Peaceful Mitchell* **(1976)**
"Davy Crockett's Tennessee Mounted Volunteers . . . died defending the 'Pallisade' wall of the Alamo."

Tinkle, Lon: *13 Days to Glory* **(1958)**
"Now, like Travis, Crockett died outdoors, where he wished to be. In mute testimony to a man whose marksmanship was legendary, the greatest concentration of Mexican bodies is said to have been found around Crockett's body."

Todish, Tim J. and Terry S.: *A Comprehensive Guide to the Alamo and the Texas Revolution* **(1998)**
"No one will dispute the fact that there were five, six, or possibly even seven Alamo defenders who were executed at the end of the battle. However, to say UNEQUIVOCALLY that Crockett was among this group simply cannot be proven at this time."

Vaughan, Robert: *Texas Glory: An Epic of the Alamo* **(1996)**
"Then Sam saw a Mexican lieutenant come up behind Crockett and slash him just above the eye with a ferocious blow from his sword."

Venable, Clarke: *All the Brave Rifles* **(1929)**
"It is enough to know that every man died at his post and that their death lifted Texas from its apathy and lighted the beacon of liberty and independence."

Vernon-Cole, Willis: *The Star of the Alamo* **(1926)**
"Uriah and Crockett clubbing muskets, piled the ground before the altar with dead. Crockett fell."

Warren, Robert Penn: *Rememer the Alamo!* **(1958)**
"Upon being hit, he seized his rifle in his left hand and leaped to the middle of the room for space to swing it. But he was now open for a Mexican volley, and fell."

Wright, Mrs. S. J.: *Our Living Alamo* **(1937)**
"Davy Crockett, 'mighty hunter of the West,' died in the corner near the church, piles of slain about him."

The last moments of Davy Crockett, illustrated by Gary Zaboly.

— From the collection of Glenn Nolan

CONCLUSION

The legend of Davy Crockett continues into yet another century—and that's something quite unique, especially when one considers that he was, essentially, a semi-literate, backwoods hunter who spent most of his life in and out of debt.

New books and a major motion picture are in the works; membership in the Direct Descendants of David Crockett continues to grow; Baby Boomers actively collect Crockett memorabilia from the 1950s; and articles about the famous frontier hero continue to fill the pages of *The Alamo Journal* and other historical publications.

Despite the ongoing interest in the Crockett of popular culture, one hopes that the Crockett of history—the man who stood up for unpopular causes because he thought he was right—will be the Crockett that Americans in the twenty-first century embrace.

Above all, when we have to make important choices in our lives, let's remember the motto of Davy Crockett: "Be sure you're right, then go ahead."

Select Bibliography

Abbott, John S. C. *David Crockett: His Life and Adventures*. New York: Dodd, Mead, 1874.

Allen, Charles Fletcher. *David Crockett, Scout, Small Boy, Pilgrim, Mountaineer, Soldier, Bear-Hunter, and Congressman, Defender of the Alamo*. Philadelphia: J. B. Lippincott, 1911.

Anderson, Paul F. *The Davy Crockett Craze*. Hillside, IL: R & G Productions, 1996.

Baugh, Virgil E. *Rendezvous at the Alamo: Highlights in the Lives of Bowie, Crockett, & Travis*. New York: Pageant Press, 1960.

Brown, Dee. *Wave High the Banner: A Novel Based on the Life of Davy Crockett*. Philadelphia: Macrae-Smith, 1942.

Burke, James Wakefield. *David Crockett: The Man Behind the Myth*. Austin, TX: Eakin Press, 1984.

Crockett, David. *A Narrative of the Life of David Crockett of the State of Tennessee*. Philadelphia: Carey & Hart, 1834.

Davis, William C. *Three Roads to the Alamo: The Lives and Fortunes of David Crockett, James Bowie, and William Barret Travis*. New York: Harper Collins, 1998.

Dorson, Richard M. *Davy Crockett: American Comic Legend*. New York: Spiral Press for Rockland Editions, 1939.

Eggleston, George Cary. *David Crockett*. New York: Dodd, Mead Company, 1875.

Ellis, Edward S. *The Life of Colonel David Crockett*. Philadelphia: Porter & Coates, 1884.

Feely, Thomas F., Jr. and Nancy E. Nagle. *Crockett's Last Stand— A Diorama*. Historical Dioramas, Inc: Ridgefield Park, NJ, 1995

Foreman, Gary L. *Crockett: The Gentleman from the Cane: A Com-*

prehensive View of the Folkhero Americans Thought They Knew. Dallas, TX: Taylor Publishing Company, 1986.

Garland, Hamlin, ed. *The Autobiography of David Crockett.* New York: Charles Scribner's Sons, 1923.

Groneman, Bill. *Death of a Legend.* Plano, TX: Republic of Texas Press, 1999.

————. *Defense of a Legend: Crockett and the de la Peña Diary.* Plano, TX: Republic of Texas Press, 1994.

Hauck, Richard Boyd. *Crockett: A Bio-Bibliography.* Westport, CT: Greenwood Press, 1982.

Judd, Cameron. *Crockett of Tennessee: A Novel Based on the Life and Times of David Crockett.* New York: Bantam Books, 1994.

Kilgore, Dan. *How Did Davy Die?* College Station: Texas A&M University Press, 1978.

Lofaro, Michael A., and Joe Cummings, eds. *Crockett at Two Hundred: New Perspectives on the Man and the Myth.* Knoxville, University of Tennessee Press, 1989.

Lofaro, Michael A. *Davy Crockett: The Man, The Legend, The Legacy, 1786-1986.* Knoxville, University of Tennessee Press, 1985.

Mayer, Edwin Justus. *Sunrise in My Pocket, Or The Last Days of Davy Crockett: An American Saga.* New York: Julian Messner, 1941.

McKernan, Frank. *David Crockett–Scout.* New York: J. B. Lippincot Company, 1921.

Meine, Franklin J., ed. *The Crockett Almanacks: Nashville Series, 1835-1838.* Chicago: The Caxton Club, 1955.

Null, Marion Michael. *The Forgotten Pioneer, The Life of Davy Crockett.* New York: Vantage Press, 1954.

Rourke, Constance. *Davy Crockett.* New York: Harcourt, 1934.

Shackford, James Atkins. *David Crockett: The Man and the Legend.* Chapel Hill: University of North Carolina Press, 1956.

Sprague, William C. *Davy Crockett.* New York: The Macmillan Company, 1915.